# LIGHT
# LOVE
# RITUALS

## RONESA AVEELA

BENDIDEIA
PUBLISHING

# Dedication

This book is dedicated to two special women.

To Viola Simpanen Florence, who loved her children more than anything else in the world and gave them the freedom and encouragement to be the people they wanted to be. We thank her for all the stories she told her children and the special ones she wrote for them. Her stories never got published and are now lost forever, but her memory lives on in the hearts of those who loved her.

To Violeta Jeliazkova, friend and founder of the Bulgarian-American Cultural Center Madara, for her support and unstoppable energy, smiles, and enthusiasm in bringing wonderful cultural Bulgarian rituals and celebrations to us throughout the years.

# Contents

# Acknowledgments

I would like to thank Radio Bulgaria, the Internet program of the Bulgarian National Radio, for a starting place for information on Bulgarian rituals and customs. Their website has a wealth of knowledge about Bulgarian history, culture, traditions, and folklore. From there, I was able to dig further into other resources.

Many thanks for my critiquers, who provided wonderful insight into ways to make the information more readable and enjoyable. Alexander Qi, Aliya Smyth, Erin Merrill, and Jordan Phillips, thank you for continuing to believe in me.

**Thrace (around 342 B.C.) in Relation to Today's Countries**

# Introduction

Bulgarians take pride in their heritage and culture, which is rich in colorful folklore and traditions. The nation practices more than ten thousand rites from a person's birth through his death. Many of these date back to an era when people both feared and worshiped nature. In the process of writing *Mystical Emona: Soul's Journey*, I found myself asking "Why?" on numerous occasions. Why did people do the things they did? Those "whys" resulted in further research. What were the origins of these customs and rituals? What did they mean?

What I discovered was an overlap of pagan and Christian beliefs. Many customs originated in the days when Thracians inhabited the area that is now modern-day Bulgaria, Greece, and Turkey. So much of the material I read said Bulgarian traditions had Thracian origins, but few articles delved into what those Thracian beliefs actually were. So I continued digging.

This book is a summation of many months spent researching. Although I did search for reliable sources to validate the claims articles made, *Light Love Rituals* is not meant to be a scholarly document. Nor is it an exhaustive study of rituals. Its purpose is to provide readers with a glimpse into Bulgarian culture. It's information I found interesting and wanted to share, so other people could take the same journey to discover the way others live and believe.

Why call it *Light Love Rituals*?

**LIGHT**: One of the main characters in rituals and folklore is the sun. In antiquity, people believed that each year the sun died and was born again. Revived, it woke nature in the spring to begin a new cycle of life.

**LOVE**: The progression of human life mirrors that of nature—birth, death, and rebirth in a different form. Where it differs is that while the sun is essential to the cycle of nature, love is what's important for human growth. Rituals reflect a family's love from a child's birth, to marriage ceremonies, to rites performed to honor the dead. Many rituals are for fertility, protection, health, and fortune.

**RITUALS**: Everyone incorporates some sort of rituals into their lives. Rituals provide an occasion for families to gather around the table and share a good meal, memories, love, and traditions from generation to generation. Rituals connect the past with the present, and help people embrace and understand their future.

*Light Love Rituals* describes traditions that are part of the story of *Soul's Journey*. Even though ancient Thracians themselves may have long been forgotten, generations of families have kept these traditions alive since Thrace was a thriving nation. Although much of the content is common knowledge among those who practice these beliefs, I hope even they will discover something new to pass on to future generations.

The chapters are divided by seasons, to reflect the relationship of nature to mankind. Each ritual begins with an overview of the custom, followed by information about its origins. Then, to make the rituals more personal and real, you can celebrate the holidays with a fictional Bulgarian family. If you've read *Soul's Journey*, you may recognize Maria. This is the story of her family. The events take place thirteen years earlier than the ones in *Soul's Journey*.

The rituals, as described here, are a collection of ceremonies practiced throughout the country. They are not representative of any one region. Today, some, like fire-dancing, are performed mainly as tourist attractions; others are a compilation of traditions found in various parts of the country.

Mixed in with the rituals are legends, related information, and fun "facts." At least for the moment, suspend your beliefs and imagine you live among people who once believed, or perhaps still do, that spirits, vampires, and ancient gods existed.

To enjoy an even greater taste of Bulgaria, try some of the recipes in the section called "Maria's Kitchen," where you can prepare popular dishes. No finer tradition exists than making Bulgarian cuisine, which is as rich as the soul of the people. The meals, like the colors woven into the nation's rugs, represent the hospitality and rich spirituality of its people. From the mystical Rhodope Mountains, the birthplace of Orpheus, to the Thracian Valley, known for its roses, whether the dishes are light or hearty, they will always be savory. Some of the recipes have a modern twist to make them easier and more interesting.

# Winter Rituals

# Budni Vecher

December 24 – Бъдни вечер – Budni vecher: Christmas Eve or Small Christmas.
December 25 – Коледа – Koleda: Christmas.
*In the Eastern Orthodox Church, the Christmas season starts on November 15 and continues until December 27, Saint Stefan's Day.*

Christmas Eve. The year is coming to a close. It's a time of festivity for Christian and non-Christian alike. In the Eastern Orthodox Church, **Budni vecher** marks the end of forty days of fasting from meat to purify both body and soul. In preparation for the holiday, families thoroughly cleanse and tidy their houses, because on *Koleda*, Christmas, traditional beliefs prohibit sweeping, washing, cleaning, and any kind of household work. An old superstition says that even sewing isn't allowed, to prevent family members from going blind.

A more unusual "cleansing" is the removal of bad spirits. To accomplish this, the female head of household walks around the home and yard with burning incense, to chase those spirits away. This tradition began long ago when people believed unseen beings lurked in dark corners. By ridding their homes of both dirt and spirits, families can greet the new year clean and full of positive energy.

Other traditions people perform on this day also have special meanings. Among these are cutting a *budnik* or Yule log, selecting food for the evening meal, and blessing families with incantations and songs.

## ~ ORIGINS ~

People in antiquity believed the winter solstice brought beginnings, rather than endings. Up until this date, the Sun was a dying god, his light shining less each day. On the solstice, however, the Sun was reborn as a new god called *Mlada Boga* or Young God, and daylight once again increased.

Various religions celebrated the solstice in their own way. In the third century A.D., Emperor Aurelian combined these celebrations into a single festival called the "Birthday of the Unconquered Sun," observed on December 25. Eventually, the early church designated this day as the celebration of the birth of Christ, and "Young God" came to refer to Jesus rather than a pagan, or non-Christian, deity.

### *Did you know...?*

*Spirits cannot cast spells using bread and wine because these items symbolize the body and blood of Christ. In fact, these sacred items frighten demons.*

[1]

During the solstice, people in antiquity believed the heavens and Earth were at their closest points and merged, renewing natural energies. With the release of this power, vile spirits and the souls of the dead

---

[1] Note: The "Did you know...?" sections highlight traditional beliefs and interesting facts from Bulgarian culture. All of them are not meant to be taken as the absolute truth. Believe what you will.

had free rein to mingle with people. These unsavory beings desired to bring chaos to the world by preventing the return of light, that is, the rebirth of the Sun God. People therefore performed rituals to protect families and crops.

## ~ RITUALS IN PRACTICE ~

*Instead of describing each ritual in detail, we invite you into the home of a fictional family, so you can celebrate with them. Let's now meet Maria and Georgi, who live in Emona, a small village in Bulgaria along the Black Sea. They have two children: eight-year-old Nikolay, whom everyone calls Niki, and his fifteen-year-old sister Rada. You'll also meet Baba Marta, Georgi's mother, who lives with the family. The children adore her, and love to listen to her stories. And we can't forget the children's puppy, Balkan. He's a Bulgarian Shepherd, also called a Karakachan.*

Early in the morning, Rada makes a fortune bread. She mixes flour into the wet dough with a spoon, then glances at her mother who's sitting at the kitchen table. "Did you used to make the *pitka*[2] when you were young, before you were engaged to Dad?"

Maria looks up from writing on slips of paper. "Yes, I always started the dough. My mother told me that having the yeast's fermentation on my hands ensured everyone in the house could eventually have children."

"I thought that's why you touched the fruit trees with the dough."

"True, we do that so women can conceive, but the ritual ensures our land stays fertile, too. It'll make sure our apple and plum trees have plenty of fruit, our garden has lots of vegetables, and the grapes in your father's vineyard are fat in the fall."

Rada continues mixing the dough. "I like making this. Maybe I can do it all next time."

"That would be helpful. I have to finish the bread today, but you can make the *tikvenik* later."

"Sure." Rada adds more flour to the dough. When it's firm enough to knead with her fingers, she says, "You can take over now, Mom."

"Thank you. I've finished writing the fortunes for the *pitka*. Will you wrap them in foil?"

"After I read them. I want to see which one I might get."

Maria trades places with Rada and works the rest of the flour into the dough. She sets it aside to rise, then goes outside. Rada joins her.

With the sticky dough still clinging to her fingers, Maria touches the fruit trees in their yard and prays, "Lord, please give us a bountiful harvest this year."

"Is asking God's help part of the ritual?"

"No, but it doesn't hurt. Before you were born, every time I did this, I asked Him to let me have children." Maria grins at Rada. "And here you and Niki are."

**Spirit Removal**

Once inside, Maria cleans her fingers, then kneels at the fireplace. She grasps a hot coal with tongs and drops it into a pan on top of *tamiyan*. The fragrant scent of incense fills the room. She carries the pan to the next room. Niki tags along, clinging to his mother's apron as she walks through each room.

He looks into dark corners and pushes smoke toward them. "Are you sure this will chase away bad spirits?"

She pats his head. "Yes. You can sleep well tonight and think about what St. Nicholas will bring you tomorrow."

---

[2] See recipes for *pitka, banitsa, tikvenik, sarmi,* and others in "Maria's Kitchen."

Satisfied she's cleansed the house, Maria heads back outside where more spirits linger. Niki scrambles from window to window, watching as his mother walks around the house. When she returns, he rushes toward her. "Mom, I saw black shapes running away when the smoke got near them."

"Really?" She arches her brows, then places the incense on a low table, where the family will eat the evening meal. "I hope I got rid of them all."

### The *Budnik*

In the forest, Georgi carries an axe over his shoulder. He looks for a young, straight oak. Last year, he felled an apple tree that no longer bore fruit. He trudges toward an oak and walks around it, inspecting the trunk. "Yes, this will do," he says. He chops it down, but doesn't allow the section he'll use as a *budnik*, or Yule log, to touch the ground, so its magical power doesn't seep into the soil. At home he carves a small hole into the trunk's long side with a chisel and hammer. He leaves the trunk on the porch and goes inside to relax before finishing the ritual.

When the sun sets, Georgi prepares the *budnik*. He pours incense, oil, and wine into the hole. Then he plugs it, wraps it in a white cloth, and brings it inside. Upon entering, he calls out, "Do you glorify the Young God?" To which his family replies, "Yes, we glorify the Young God. We welcome him."

## Did you know...?

Budnik *ashes and embers possess magical healing powers. Scattering them over fields ensures crops are plentiful, and mixing them with feed makes livestock healthy and fertile. In some villages, people sprinkle ashes in a hen's nest hoping the bird will lay more eggs.*

Georgi removes the white cloth, then places the log into the fireplace with the plugged end on top. Niki comes over and sits on the hearth. "Can I help?"

"Sure. You can take the plug out, while I get matches to light the *budnik*."

Niki grasps the plug and yanks on it until his father returns. "I think it's stuck."

"I guess I put it in too tight." Georgi wraps his hands around Niki's. The two pull together until the plug pops out. He hands his son a match. "You can light it."

Niki peers into the hole, then sniffs it. "It's like what Mom burned earlier. Will this keep spirits away, too?"

Georgi chuckles. "No, it's to make sure everyone stays healthy. When the *budnik* burns, it sends energy toward the sun. In return, the sun protects us."

"Isn't the sun already hot enough? It doesn't need more energy."

"It's a different kind of energy. The *budnik*'s fire symbolizes the sun's heat, light, and ability to ensure life. We let it burn all night so its energy helps with the sun's rebirth at the solstice. You can ask Baba to tell you one of her stories about the sun being reborn every year."

### The Meal

Maria inserts the foil-wrapped fortunes into the *pitka* when the dough has risen, then she places the pan into the oven. Soon its mouth-watering aroma drifts throughout the house. While the bread bakes, Rada removes filo dough from the refrigerator for *tikvenik*, a pumpkin *banitsa*. Maria gets the ingredients to make *sarmi*, stuffed grape leaves, and *oshav*, boiled dry apples and plums.

Niki rushes over, with Balkan behind him. "Let me help, too."

Maria points toward the cupboard. "You can get mixed nuts, honey, apples, plums, and dried fruit, and put them into the dishes on the table."

He rubs his finger over the colorful design baked into the clay bowls. "These are the ones you bought in the market this week."

"That's right. We all got something new for the house, so we'll have good luck."

Niki retrieves the requested items, and eats a few nuts while he pours them into the bowl. He counts the dishes for the feast, starting with the ones he placed on the table. "One, two, three, four, five." He looks at Rada rolling up the *tikvenik* log. "Six." Then he turns toward his mother and counts the *sarmi* and *oshav*. "Seven, eight." And finally he looks at the oven and breathes in deep. "Nine." He points at each item, counting them again. "Only nine this year?"

"No, silly, twelve," Rada replies as she ruffles his hair. "I'll take out red wine, olives, and garlic later. We used to have only seven or nine before Baba moved in, but you were too young to remember that."

"Why does it matter how many we have?" Niki pops more nuts into his mouth.

Maria answers from the sink, where she's washing grape leaves. "We make sure we have seven, nine, or twelve dishes because those are special numbers. Seven is magical, nine is how many months a baby grows, and twelve signifies the months of the year."

Niki peeks into the oven when Rada checks the bread. "The dough grapes on top of the *pitka* are so golden. Why do we have grapes on top anyway?"

"You have lots of questions today," she says. "That's what Dad does for work. Since he grows grapes, we decorate the *pitka* with them." She places the bread on top of the stove to cool. "Farmers decorate theirs with ploughs, like your friend Yordan's family. My friend Helena prefers to have a cross and other religious symbols on top."

Niki sticks his nose close to the bread. "Mmm. I love this." He moves out of the way when his sister puts the *tikvenik* and *sarmi* into the oven. "And both of those, too. Next year I want to help."

"You can help now by telling Dad and Baba we'll be ready in about half an hour."

"Can I help Dad with the straw?" He jiggles from foot to foot.

"Go check," Maria says. "I think he's resting in his room."

Niki dashes away, returning moments later, handfuls of straw clutched close to his chest. "I'm helping Dad!"

Georgi and Niki spread the straw in front of the hearth. Over the straw, Georgi sets a *sinia*, the low, wooden table Maria had placed the incense on earlier.

"Dad?" Niki sits on exposed straw. "Why aren't we putting the cloth down like we did last year?"

"It was too difficult for Baba to get up from sitting on the floor. Remember?"

Niki puts his hand over his mouth to stop the laughter because Baba enters the room. He kisses both her cheeks when she sits in her rocker. "I know why we put straw on the floor."

"You do?" She pretends she doesn't know why. "Please tell me."

"It's because Jesus was born in a stable."

"That's right." Baba rocks in her chair. "And do you know what we do with the straw afterwards?"

"Umm, burn it around the fruit trees?"

"Not quite. Your dad will scatter some under the fruit trees, and burn the rest in the vineyard."

Niki looks at his dad, then back to his grandmother. "Why does he do that?"

"He puts it under the trees so they'll produce more fruit, and he burns some in the vineyard to protect the grapes from hailstorms." Baba leans forward and motions for Niki to come closer. She whispers, "And do you know what your mother did when she had you in her belly?"

"No," he whispers back.

"She lay on the straw before your father took it away, so you'd be born healthy."

Niki stares at his mother. "Mom, is—"

Maria puts her finger to her lips. "Niki, you can help set the table. Everything's ready."

He skips over and picks up the nuts, eating another one.

## Did you know...?

*Cracking a walnut and finding plump meat inside means you'll be healthy and successful for the year. But, beware, if it's shriveled, you'll suffer illness and have bad luck.*

When they finish setting the table, everyone sits on three-legged wooden chairs.

Georgi breaks the bread into chunks, wraps the first piece in a white cloth, and sets it aside.

Niki reaches for it. "Can I have that one?"

"No," his father says. "That's for the entire household." He breaks off two more pieces and places them on a plate. "This one's for God and the Virgin Mary, and the other one is for Balkan."

"Balkan can't eat it." Niki pouts. "Why does he get a piece before me?"

"He has to have a fortune, too. You can eat his piece later if you want."

"Yes, I do." Niki smiles.

Finally, Georgi passes a piece to every family member, beginning with Baba, then Maria, Rada, and finally Niki.

Niki smashes his piece, looking for the foil-covered treasure hidden inside. "I hope I get the coin so I'll be the luckiest one this year." He unwraps the foil and sighs. "Nope. It's a fortune. 'You will grow tall and strong this year.' Yeah! I'm going to be as tall as Dad."

Baba breaks in. "Did anyone get the coin?"

Everyone says, "No," at the same time.

Niki wiggles in his seat. "Can I check the others, pleeeease."

"Go ahead." His mother hands him the plate. "Check the house one first."

After he tears it apart, he shouts, "The coin's here. Yeah! We're all going to be healthy and lucky this year. I'm going to eat this piece  and save mine to put under my pillow."

Baba puts her hand on Niki's. "I hope you have a wonderful dream. *Budni vecher* dreams are certain to become reality." She winks at Rada. "And perhaps you'll dream of a nice young man."

"Baba, no! If I do, I'll have to marry him this year, and I'm not ready for that." Rada blushes. "I still want to participate in the *lazaruvane* this spring and wear flowers in my hair, and all the other fun things we do on *Tsvenitsa*."

Balkan whines, nosing in between each person.

"Someone should let the dog out while we eat." Georgi looks at Maria, who arches her eyebrows.

"What?" she says. "You know we can't get up once the meal's started. Only the head of household, and that's you."

He chuckles. "Of course. We don't want to chance having bad luck." He stoops as he walks toward the door.

Niki tugs on his grandmother's sleeve. "Baba, something's wrong with Dad."

"Nothing to worry about." She smiles at him. "It's customary to walk bent over if we have to leave the table. It represents heavy grains of wheat on the stalk. We do it to make sure the harvest is plentiful."

When the family finishes their meal, Niki says, "I'll help clean up."

"Not tonight," Maria says. "We leave food out all night so our ancestors' spirits can eat their fill."

"But ..." Niki purses his lips. "I thought you got rid of all the spirits."

"Yes, dear, I did. The bad ones. Our ancestors are good spirits, who protect us, not harm us."

## The *Koledari* Blessings

Later that evening, Niki's friend Yordan Dimitrov stops by with his father Adrian. "Niki, I'm so excited to be in the *Koleduvane* procession this year. Are you?"

"Yes." Niki puts on his jacket, then grabs his traditional folk costume from the chair. "Let's go. Bye, Mom, Dad, Baba, Rada. See you later."

They say their own good-byes and wait for the carolers to return.

"Our little boy is growing up." Maria sighs.

"At least it's no longer an initiation rite," Baba says. "He's not ready to go out on his own and start a family."

"No, but my little warrior thinks he has the power to battle spirits that bring winter's cold."

Soon after midnight, the parade of boys and bachelors makes its way back to Niki's house. Niki and Yordan walk in front, shouting, "The *koledari* are coming," as loud as they can. They swing their carved walking sticks, which are decorated with flowers and popcorn. Several ring-shaped buns dangle around the top of their staffs. The bags at their sides are stuffed with coins, walnuts, bacon, sausage, and cheese that they've received in return for blessings they've given at each home. The men also carry a *baklitsa*, a small, wooden flask of wine, used on special occasions.

As the leader, Adrian knocks on the door and is the first to enter. He raises his *baklitsa* and recites a blessing: "Health from God. Merriment from us." Then he drinks a toast.

The *koledari* gather around him and sing, "Welcome us. We sing for you, dear hosts. We are kind guests visiting. Kind guests, *koledari*."

They sing other traditional songs and recite incantations about health, well-being, and happiness for both the house and its occupants. Maria and Georgi give each of them gifts, which the singers add to their nearly full bags.

After the *koledari* say good-bye, Niki runs back inside as his father is about to close the door. He wraps his arms around his mother and quickly says, "Bye, Mom!" He rushes to catch up with the other singers, who are proceeding to the next house to give their blessings and receive more gifts.

# Survaki

**January 1 – Сурваки – Survaki: New Year's.**
Koleda *and* Survaki *border the old and new year. Both holidays fall within the "Dirty Days," the time between Ignatius Feast on December 20 and the Epiphany on January 6. During this time, the Virgin Mary went into labor, gave birth to Jesus, and had him baptized.*

*This is also a day the Orthodox Church honors the memory of St. Basil. This devoted theologian did much work to care for the poor and underprivileged. He also dedicated himself to creating guidelines for the community life, prayer, and labor of monks. Born 330 A.D. Died January 1, 379 A.D.*

**St. Basil**

On **Survaki**, people party and ring in the new year, but like many Bulgarian holidays, other rituals ensure good health, fertility, and wealth. The day is especially exciting for children. They participate in the fun-filled tradition of creating a *survachka* stick. Although girls decorate this cornel branch along with boys, it is bachelors and boys between four and twelve years old who travel from house to house with the *survachka*. When they arrive, they tap family and friends on the back with the stick to bestow blessings on them. They also tap livestock and domestic animals to ensure they remain healthy and fertile. In return, the boys receive gifts from the family.

## ~ ORIGINS ~

In antiquity, *Survaki* was a time to move away from darkness toward light as days became longer. The festival gets its name from the Thracian god Sureget, also called Surgast, Suroter, or Surat, all meaning "glorious sun."[3] Many nations besides Thrace worshipped the Sun God. In India believers called him Surya (from the Aryans who conquered that nation), and the Thracian's northern neighbors, the Scythians, called him Getosur.

The *survachka* branch itself has ancient origins. Made of cornel, it was one of the sacred World Trees. People believed that by performing mystical rituals, they could transfer the branch's magic to those who held it, giving them prosperity, health, and long life. Equipped with this power, they could communicate with heaven and the underworld, acting as mediators between this life and the next one.

## *Did you know...?*

*Sycamores and walnuts are World Trees. The difference between them is that it's safe to sleep only in a sycamore's shade. Samodivi, Bulgarian woodland nymphs, like to gather by walnut trees. If they find you asleep there, they can make you become ill.*

---

[3] Serafimov, Pavel, "Surva, Bulgarian Sourvakars Divine Light" (translated), Dec. 29, 2014, http://sparotok .blogspot.com/2014/12/blog-post_29.html?m=1.

# What Is a World Tree?

*Ancient civilizations considered nature sacred, and they deeply venerated the World Tree as a force of strength and protection. The three parts of the tree symbolize the nature of the universe. Branches represent the heavens where divine spirits reside. The trunk signifies Earth, which is the home of men and preternatural creatures like nymphs and fairies. And roots represent the underworld and the dead who dwell there. Like nature itself, all these creatures live in harmony with one another. Also demonstrating the world's unity were Thracian deities, who performed their designated functions, working together as a triad, none having dominion over the others.*

## ~ RITUALS IN PRACTICE ~

On the eve of *Survaki*, Maria and Rada scurry around, setting the table with food similar to the *Budni vecher* meal. Tonight the additional aroma of meat fills the air.

Niki dances around, singing, "Christmas Lent is over. No more fasting!"

"Hey there, you can help if you want." Rada hands him a few twigs. "Put these around the table. Okay?"

"I'm glad we're going to eat at the big table, instead of the low one we put over hay." He pokes at the buds, then lays them by the various dishes. He sniffs the bread. "Mmm. More *pitka*, but it's decorated different this time. No grapes on top. It's like this twig instead."

His mother hands him utensils. "The design's a cornel branch, which protects us and keeps us healthy."

"I know I'm going to get the coin this time." Niki places a fork by his plate, then puts the others around each place setting.

Rada leans against a chair. "Or maybe you'll find the cornel twig in the foil. It would be better if you were healthy and protected, the way you jump around. Let's hope Dad gets the coin, so he'll earn lots this year."

Maria shoos Niki away. "Please go get your father and Baba. We're ready to eat."

When everyone is seated, Maria lights incense and spreads the smoke over the table in a circular motion from left to right.

Niki turns to Baba. "Is this more protection?"

"Yes, dear. It's important to have protection so we don't get sick."

Maria spins the plate the *pitka*'s on three times. "Baba, you can take the first piece."

Baba looks at it, then bends closer to Niki. "Which piece should I break off?"

He bites his thumbnail, then points. "This one, I think. Then me next, please."

"Go ahead," his mother says.

Surva, surva year,
A merry year,
Golden wheat in the field,
Red apples in the orchard,
Plump grains of wheat in the field,
A house full of silk,
A large cluster of grapes on the vine,
Live healthy next year,
Till next year, Amen!

Each member of the family takes a piece to discover his fortune. This time Rada gets the coin, and Georgi gets the cornel twig. The others read their fortunes out loud.

Maria laughs. " 'You will find true love.' " She hands it to Rada. "I've already found mine. I think you should have this one. I saw that boy looking your way at church this morning."

Before Rada can respond, Baba unwraps her fortune. " 'Health and wealth all year long.' "

Finally Niki reads his. " 'You will have an exciting adventure.' Yeah!"

**Making the *Survachka***

After the meal is over, Niki asks, "Are we going to make the *survachka* now?"

Maria wipes crumbs off the table into her hand. "As soon as we put all the food away."

"We're not leaving it out for our ancestors tonight?"

"No, they don't get food this holiday."

"The ancestors don't get food tonight. That means more for *me* later," Niki chants while he helps clean up.

When they're done, Maria says, "You can get your coat and go outside with Rada now. She'll cut a cornel twig for you."

"We're making *survachka*! We're making *survachka*!"

Rada rolls her eyes. "Was I this annoying when I was his age?"

Maria smiles. "No, you were much too serious."

"Come along, Niki." Rada, with pruning shears in hand, steps out into the cold.

Niki runs to the tree and searches for the right-sized branch. "I want that one." He points to a spot too high for him to reach.

Rada cuts the branch, then one for herself.

"Why do we always make them from cornel?" Niki inspects his branch, snapping off small twigs.

"The wood's strong and can withstand the cold, and it's easy to bend when it's still green. Before we moved here, we sometimes cut twigs from apple or plum trees instead."

## *Did you know...?*

*Cornel wood is powerful enough to use as a stake to kill vampires.*

Back inside, Rada and Niki sit at the table with Baba. Niki bounces in his seat.

Baba smiles. "If you don't sit still, you're going to knock decorations onto the floor, and Balkan will eat them."

Niki looks at Rada. She's already tied yarn around the side twigs so they form a circle in the middle, and now she's twisting a red strand around the bottom. Niki bends the twigs on his own branch, but they slip out of his fingers. He tries again, but the branches snap back. Discouraged, he drops the twig onto the table. "Baba, will you help me?"

"That's why I'm here." She picks up the branch and bends a twig on each side toward the center, then holds them in place. "Cut a small piece of yarn and wrap it around the branch, starting here." She points with her free hand.

He follows her step-by-step instructions until he secures the two side twigs into a circle around the main branch. "Thank you, Baba." He kisses her cheek. "Now how should I decorate it?"

"First you want to cover all the wood with yarn. Your sister has red. Do you want to use that or another color? You can do each section a different color. Your mom left us green, blue, orange, yellow, black, and white."

Niki looks over the yarn. "I'll use blue first."

"Start at the bottom. I'll hold the branch tight so it won't move."

With deep concentration, Niki winds yarn around the base and ties it when he reaches the circle.

"All these decorations have different meanings," Baba says. "Yarn represents health, happiness, and life that binds families together."

"I'm glad you're my family." Niki leans closer and whispers, "But I'm not always sure about Rada."

His sister looks down her nose at him, then says, "Mine's done!" She holds out her *survachka*. Dried fruit, threads, a coin, pretzels, strings of popcorn, and more items decorate the branch.

"Lovely." Baba points to items on the *survachka*. "Each of these has different meanings. Dried fruit, red peppers, pretzels, and popcorn symbolize fertility. As I've probably told you many times, fertile soil meant a good harvest. Without plenty of crops, our ancestors would starve."

"Yes, Baba, you've told us that *lots* of times." Rada gets up from the table. "But we still love you." She bends to kiss her grandmother.

"Baba, will you help me decorate the rest of mine so it's as colorful as Rada's?"

"Yes, Niki. Let's see what you can put on next." She searches the assortment of decorations. "I'll string popcorn. While I do that, you can tie a mini bagel on top."

They add more decorations until the branch is completely covered.

Niki twirls the finished *survachka*. "Thank you, Baba. I love it!" He gets up to show his mother. "Look at mine. I have wool, colored paper, threads, seeds, raisins, walnuts, a bagel, dried fruit." He stops to take a breath. "And a Chinese coin. Baba says some of these things ..." He pauses and speaks more slowly, "represent a family's livelihood." He taps a coin wrapped in green yarn. "She told me this will make double sure I have a prosperous new year."

Maria examines her son's creation. "It's as unique and spirited as you are, Niki."

## The *Survakari* Blessing

Early the next morning, Niki and his friend Yordan join other boys and young, unmarried men from the village. Simeon, a neighbor, leads these *survakari* from house to house, singing and giving blessings to all the families.

Niki looks around. "We've walked in a circle around the village."

"That's right," Simeon says. "The route symbolizes the path the sun takes in the sky."

"So?" Niki asks. "Why do we have to follow the sun?"

"Our ancestors, the Thracians, believed the sun would protect them, so the route they took was symbolic of the sun. Something like that, I think. My baba tells me all kinds of stories."

"Mine, too." Niki swings his *survachka* as if tapping someone with it. He turns to Yordan and whispers close to his ear. They both laugh.

After they arrive at Niki's house, the youths sing songs about well-being and prosperity. Niki and the others head toward the fireplace where his family has gathered. Niki nudges Yordan. "Baba says the spirits of our ancestors gather here."

"I know. Same at my house."

Niki taps Baba on the shoulder with his *survachka* and recites a blessing for prosperity: "Surva, surva year; a merry year; golden wheat in the field; red apples in the orchard; plump grains of wheat in the field; a house full of silk; a large cluster of grapes on the vine; live healthy next year; till next year, Amen!"

He continues blessing the rest of his family in order of age: Georgi, Maria, and ending with Rada. He taps her harder than the others, then backs away when she glares at him. He whispers to Yordan, "I told you I dared to hit her hard."

With the ritual tapping of the elders over, Maria and Georgi give the boys gifts of money, sweets, and fruits in return for their blessings.

# Making a Survachka

*Branch from cornel wood tree
   or any other tree*
*Colorful yarn (preferably earth colors:
   red, green, orange, yellow, and brown)*

*Unbuttered, popped popcorn*
*Dried fruit*
*A round pretzel or a small bagel*
*A pair of scissors*

Many families get together during the winter holidays. This is a time for young and old to form bonds. While children make the *survachka*, grandparents enjoy giving instructions and explaining the meaning of each item. For children, it is a time to express their creativity.

### Tie the Branch
- Trim the base branch of leaves and extra twigs so the main limb has a branch coming off each side at the same point, about in the middle (like a plus sign).
- Select a strand of red or multicolor yarn and tie together the two small branches to form either a heart shape or a round shape (will form a φ). If the branches are thin and short, make a round shape.
- Starting from the bottom, wind the yarn around the base branch.
- Wind the yarn around the side branches.

### Add Decorations
- **Popcorn:** Make a bowl of popcorn and thread the pieces onto a length of red yarn using a needle. Place as many strings as you want on the *survachka*.
- **Dried Fruit:** Thread some dried fruit the same way as you did the popcorn, and tie it to the *survachka*. Cranberries, apricots, and raisins add a decorative touch.
- **Bagel or Pretzel:** Tie a mini bagel or a small twisted pretzel to the *survachka*.

**To make your own bagels:** Mix together 1 cup flour, 1/2 cup water, and 1 Tablespoon salt to create the dough. Add more flour or water if needed. Shape small bagels and bake them at 375˚F (190˚C) for about 20 minutes until they are golden. These are hard and are not suitable for eating; use only as decorations.

Ask your kids to help and use other decorations: Chinese coins, pompons, or artificial flowers. *"Surva Surva New Year! A lot of health and happiness!"*

# Trifonovden

**February 1 and 14 – Трифоновден – Trifonovden: St. Trifon's Day, Trifon Zarezan, or Trifon the Pruner.**
*A day to honor St. Trifon, or Trypho of Campsada. Born 225 A.D. Martyred 250 A.D. Patron of gardeners and winegrowers. Known as a healer, especially of animals. Tortured and beheaded after he converted the prefect Lucius to Christianity.*

*The holiday originally fell on February 14 in the Julian calendar. In 1968, the Bulgarian Orthodox Church introduced the Gregorian calendar. With this change, the new date became February 1. Many people now honor the saint on the first, and dedicate the fourteenth to winegrowers.*

*The grape harvest begins on September 14, the day of the Holy Cross. Even before then, on August 6, the Transfiguration of Christ, people bring grapes to church for the priest's blessing. After this consecration, they are allowed to eat grapes.*

**St. Trifon**

Wine production was as popular a Thracian occupation as it is now for their descendants. It's no wonder Bulgarians have a holiday or two centering on wine.

Although many Bulgarians don't practice every tradition in this day and age, ***Trifonovden*** is one that's quite popular, especially with men. It's a day sanctioned for them to drink freely and deal with the consequences later.

Viticulture is more than growing grapes. It's a process where people harshly prune vines so they grow stronger and the grapes fuller. In the *Trifonovden* vine-pruning ceremony, however, only a few branches are symbolically cut to mark the beginning of the agricultural season. The actual full pruning occurs the following month. Besides trimming vines, men crown a king of the vineyard. They choose him carefully, because his success is supposed to guarantee everyone's success. If the king has a bountiful harvest, so will they. On the negative side, if the king's harvest is poor, theirs will be as well.

## ~ ORIGINS ~

Many theories abound about the origins of winemaking. Scholars debate who first brought viticulture to the region of Bulgaria, Greece, and Turkey. Some speculate that when Thracians populated the area, they brought grapevines, cultivated them, and began wine production.

### Did you know...?

*Odysseus gave the Cyclops Polyphemus a popular Thracian wine to put the creature to sleep, so he could blind the one-eyed monster with his spear.*

What is less debated is that *Trifonovden* originated from spring-awakening rituals. Thracian Rozalii performed these rites in forests to celebrate Zagreus, the god of wine and fertility. People commonly associate these celebrations with Maenads, wild woman often depicted in a state of madness, who ripped

14

animals apart and ate them raw. Unmarried Thracian men (called *a-bii*, "not alive") also performed these rites at rock piles and in caves. Their singing and ritual games dealt not only with land's fertility, but also with immortality.[4] After all, Zagreus, associated with the Greek Dionysus (whom the Romans called Bacchus), was the twice-born god.

## The Twice-Born God

*The most common legend of the birth of Zagreus-Dionysus proclaims him the son of the god Zeus and a mortal, Semele (whose name means "mother earth," and is related to an old Bulgarian word "Земля," or "Zemlia," which means "earth"). Hera, wife of Zeus, became jealous and angry at the god's infidelity. She convinced Semele to have Zeus show her his true form. When he did, the splendor of his lightning bolts burned Semele to death. Zeus removed her unborn baby and sewed him into his own thigh, from where the child was eventually born.*

*In a second version, Hera ordered the Thracian tribes to remove the baby from Semele's womb and burn him. After they had done this, vines grew out of the ashes.*

*Another legend, however, says the child Zagreus-Dionysus was born to Zeus and Persephone, queen of the underworld and wife of Hades. Hera commanded the Titans to entice the child away with toys, then they tore him apart. They ate him, except for his heart, which Athena, Rhea, or Demeter saved. Zeus re-formed the child and implanted him into Semele, who gave Dionysus his second birth. Other versions say Zeus or Semele swallowed the heart and gave birth to Dionysus.*

Like ceremonies moon worshipers performed, Dionysian rituals often resulted in orgies and ended with a symbolic tearing apart of the king-priest when followers sacrificed a bull, horse, goat, or human. The participants sprinkled the sacrificial blood over the earth for fertility, as a representation of the creation of life.

Since Dionysus was the god of wine, his worshipers used this drink extensively in rituals. It gave them strength and courage, and more importantly immortality.

Priests poured wine on an altar's fire to make predictions. The height of the blaze indicated the bounty of the harvest. A myriad of flames bursting forth from the sacrificial animal indicated a year of abundance. However, if a fire was difficult to start or had few flames, a year of poverty loomed before them.

---

[4] Villa Yustina, "Thracians and wine," http://villayustina.com/index.php?option=com_content&view=article&id=33%3Ahistory&catid=6%3Aaboutus&Itemid=1&lang=en.

In silence they trod along the dark, steep slope.
Near the end, blackness transformed into gray shadows.
Joyful, he stepped into the daylight of the upper world.
Eager to see her, he tuned to gaze upon his love.
Arms extended to hold her, he grasped nothing but air.
As she disappeared into the gloomy land of death,
One faint word scarcely reached his ears:
"Farewell."

Famed lyre player Orpheus promoted the Dionysian cult, teaching the mysteries of the soul after death. A central concept of Orphism maintained that the body was an evil prison holding the divine soul captive.[5] To release an initiate's soul from his body, Orphic followers cremated him upon his death. Gold leaves buried with his ashes contained prayers and instructions for his life in the underworld.[6]

Orpheus is better known for his descent into Hades to return his wife Eurydice to the world of the living. Grieving after his new bride died when a poisonous snake bit her heel, he crossed the river Styx into the land of the dead. When he reached its rulers, Hades and Persephone, he played his lyre and sang of his love for Eurydice and how he tried to go on living without her, but failed. They, too, knew Amor's love, so he pleaded with them to return his wife. In time, they both would return to the realm of the dead. Brought to tears by his beautiful song, the underworld rulers allowed Eurydice to leave, but with a warning that Orpheus must not gaze upon her until they were back home. As they neared the top, he feared she was no longer there, and he turned to look at her. She disappeared with a faint "Farewell."

After this failed attempt at restoring his love, Orpheus spurned women and forsook the Dionysian rites to worship only Apollo, god of the sun. These actions angered the Maenads, and Orpheus suffered the same fate as Dionysus when the women tore him apart.

## ~ RITUALS IN PRACTICE ~

Long before the sun rises, Maria gets up to prepare a simple meal Georgi will take with him to the vineyard. Chicken with a bulgar stuffing, and a round, flat bread called *trifonski*. She decorates the top with an elaborate design the way she does the *pitka* on other holidays, only this time she makes images of vines and grapes.

Georgi dresses in his traditional holiday clothing, kisses Maria good-bye, and goes to church. He sits next to Adrian Dimitrov. "Your boys let you get away today?"

"They said my small patch of grapes qualifies me as a vintner," Adrian jokes.

The men become quiet when the priest enters. He reads special blessings during the service. "May grace fall on each vine," he says as he consecrates the men. Throughout the ceremony, he calls them "the vineyard of God." After the service concludes, the priest hands each man a vial of holy water to take to the fields.

Georgi says to Adrian, "I'll meet you at your house in a few minutes." He walks home, with the sun barely peeking over the horizon.

The house smells of baked chicken and bread when Georgi opens the door. "It's a good thing Niki's still asleep," he says to Maria. "I'd have a difficult time keeping him here."

---

[5] Athanassakis, Apostolos N. (trans.) and Wolkow, Benjamin M. (trans.), The Orphic Hymns. Baltimore, MD: The Johns Hopkins University Press, 2013, p. xiv.
[6] Godwin, Joscelyn, Ph.D., "The Orphic Mysteries," in The Golden Thread, Quest Books, the imprint of the Theosophical Publishing House, 2007, https://www.rosicrucian.org/publications/digest/digest1_2008/11_Godwin_The%20Orphic%20Mysteries/ONLINE_11_Godwin.pdf.

"It's no place for a boy, with all that drinking you men do." Maria hands him a new bag packed with the meal. "Enjoy yourself. Perhaps you'll be voted king this year."

"It's possible. Last year's harvest was better than I expected." He fills his *baklitsa* with wine and puts on a *kalpak*, a black, woolen cap worn specially for ceremonies.

A rosy sky greets Georgi when he picks up a sickle and pruning shears he left on the porch. He whistles while he strolls down the street toward Adrian's house. When all the men have gathered, they joke and sing songs about wine while they make their way to the vineyard.

### The Pruning Ceremony

After setting their bags, *baklitsi*, and tools on the ground, the men walk around the outside of the vineyard, holding up icons of Saint Trifon. Back at the starting point, they face east and make the sign of the cross three times.

## Did you know...?

*In Thracian times, the cross symbolized the sun. Before men ploughed their fields, they faced the sun and made the sign of the cross. This act connected people with the sun and fertility, ensuring the fruitfulness of the land.*

"Let's begin," someone says. "The sooner we do this, the quicker we can eat."

"And drink," someone else shouts.

They all laugh.

Groups of two or three men head in different directions. Georgi and Adrian walk toward a corner of the vineyard. Others have gone into the center of the field.

Georgi asks, "You want to dig or pour?"

Adrian takes a sip from his *baklitsa*. "Pour." He shakes it. "If there's any left."

Georgi laughs while he strikes the soil around the root of a large vine. When he's loosened the dirt, he sets the tool down and sips his own wine. "All yours."

Adrian kneels by the root and pours red wine around it three times. He reaches into his pocket and removes two small bags. From one, he takes a crust of bread, breaks it, and puts four pieces into the hole, equal distances apart. "How many drops in the wine, that many grapes in the vineyard this year." He opens the other bag and pours ashes into the hole.

"From your *budnik*?" Georgi asks.

"Yes. Magical ashes to make the grape harvest good again this year."

"Time to prune the vines." Georgi snips three shoots, and Adrian does the same. "My grandfather said the village priest used to come to the vineyard and prune the first vine."

"Mine says the same."

They both sprinkle the shoots with consecrated water and ashes from the *budnik*.

Adrian says, "It's nice that we're given the holy water and allowed to do it ourselves now, but it would be easier on my joints if the priest still did it."

Both men twist the three shoots into a wreath and decorate their *baklitsi* with it. Then they cut a few more shoots to take home to place by icons of the saints.

"Let's join the others so we can eat." Adrian walks toward the center of the vineyard where most of the men have already gathered.

## King of the Vineyard

The men eat and drink their fill, sing, and tell jokes and stories. In the early afternoon, when the wine and food are gone, they approach last year's "King of the vineyard." He raises his hand to quiet them. "It's time to bless our new *tsar na lozyata*."

They murmur, looking at one another, wondering who produced the most wine.

The reigning king picks up a sprig of basil and says, "Whoever is happy, let him take this bunch and be king!" Everyone trains their eyes on the sprig. The old king looks at each man, lingering before gazing at the next man. He finally walks toward Georgi and holds out the basil.

Georgi looks at it, a smile creeping up his face, now ruddy from more than wine.

# Wine Symbolism

Bulgarian celebrations revolve as much around life and fertility now as they did for the Thracians. Red wine has symbolized fertility, blood, and life since ancient times, so much so that it's an important part of major **lifecycle events** from birth through death.

- Parents symbolically leave wine at the hearth to ensure infants are healthy and have rosy cheeks.
- Wine is a staple at weddings. Newlyweds drink it before they enter their home so they'll live in love and harmony.
- Families pour wine onto graves so the earth will accept the deceased person into the ground.

Red wine accompanies many **festivals** and **special occasions** as well.

- To honor a home's guardian spirit on saint name days, people leave a glass of wine in a corner of the house.
- Builders pour wine into a home's foundation to strengthen the house.

Since red wine symbolizes blood and life, no one should drink it or even consume red food on August 29, the Feast of Seknovenie, when St. John the Baptist was beheaded.

"Come on, Georgi, take it," one of his friends encourages him.

Adrian shouts, "Maybe we should go back to the custom where the king has a large, happy family, then Dimitri would win. How many you have now?"

"Six!" the man bellows.

"I'd rather have it be Georgi," someone else says. "If we're going to share in the king's success, I'd prefer a harvest of grapes than a brood of children."

> ## Did you know...?
>
> *In Christian tradition, God created grapes. Satan, always trying to outdo Him, made blackberries. So beware if you eat blackberries before you've consumed grapes. Satan can control you, since you've had a taste of his handiwork.*

The men laugh and slap each other on the backs, while they continue to persuade Georgi to take the herbs. He finally accepts the basil.

Last year's king removes the consecrated wreath Georgi put on his *baklitsa* and places it on Georgi's head. Someone pushes a cart over, and Georgi sits in it. A couple of men push the cart out of the vineyard and toward the village.

"I'm glad you have a cart this year," Georgi says. "I'd hate to be carried and dropped by you drunken fools."

"You're God's messenger today," Adrian says. "We can't let your feet touch the ground."

Georgi chuckles. "It was my face I was worried about."

They stop at each house in the village, and Georgi blesses the families. "As the wine pours, so the vines may grow."

The hosts offer them more wine, which the men gladly accept. After everyone takes a drink, they pour the rest over Georgi.

He sputters, "The more wine poured today, the more plentiful the harvest."

When they've visited every family, Georgi says, "Come to a feast at my house tonight. I'm going to change first, then bring out my best wine."

### The Legend of Trifon and Mary

Georgi sings on his way into the house. Rada and Niki are so intent on a story Baba's telling them that they don't look up.

"Disaster once struck St. Trifon, the brother of the Virgin Mary, while he was pruning vines," Baba says.

"Did he fall off the wagon while the other men were pushing it?" Niki asks.

Baba laughs at Niki's unintended play on words. "He wasn't drinking wine, but he was rude to his sister. It was the fortieth day after the birth of Jesus, and Mary was going to the Temple to pray. Her brother mocked her for claiming God was the child's father. 'Where are you taking that child? Where's his *real* father?' Trifon yelled at her when she passed him."

Rada gasps. "He's a saint and said something like that?"

"This was before he was a saint. He was often tactless. Later, his ability to heal redeemed him of that bad attitude."

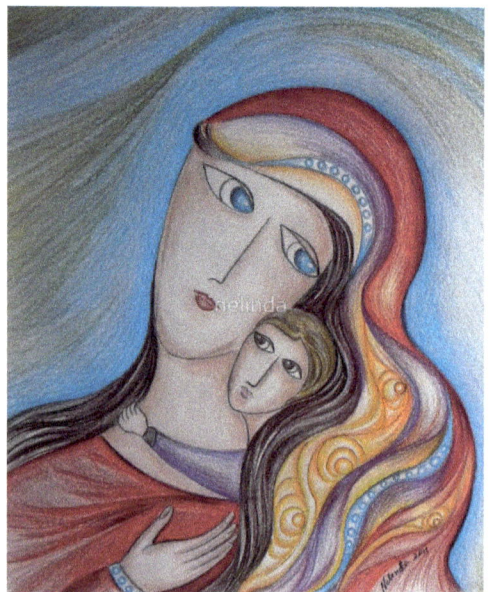

Baba waits until the children stop fidgeting. "Mary was annoyed, of course. She decided to teach her brother a lesson. When she returned to the village, she told Trifon's wife that he had cut off his nose."

Niki puts his hand on his own nose. "How'd he do that?"

"Let Baba continue, and she'll tell us," Rada says.

"Trifon's wife hurried to help him, but discovered he wasn't hurt. When she told him why she was there, he scolded her. 'You stupid woman, look. My nose is right where it's supposed to be.' He reached to touch his nose, forgetting he still held a sickle, and he cut off his nose as Mary proclaimed."

Rada giggles. "Serves him right."

"This is why women aren't allowed to go to the fields with men today," Baba says. "The men say a woman's presence would prevent the grapes from growing."

Maria comments from the kitchen. "We know it's really because they want to get drunk without us nagging them."

Georgi's loud singing from the bedroom makes them all laugh.

Maria wipes her hands on a dish towel. "Niki, I've called Yordan's mother. She says you can sleep there tonight. It's going to be a long, noisy evening here."

# WINTER: What Have You Learned?

1. **Which activity is done on** Budni vecher?
   A. Chasing away spirits from dark corners with incense.
   B. Eating meat at the evening meal.
   C. Rolling in the snow in shorts.
   D. Running around the village shooting flaming arrows.

2. **Why is the evening meal left on the table overnight on** Budni vecher?
   A. So the family pets can eat the leftovers.
   B. Because everyone is too tired from making the meal to clear it away.
   C. So the spirits of visiting ancestors can share in the family's meal while they protect the household.
   D. Because St. Nicholas came to visit.

3. **What is NOT associated with a World Tree?**
   A. God and angels.
   B. Fairies and nymphs.
   C. Ghosts and devils.
   D. Creepy crawly spiders.

4. **On** Trifonovden, **what do men put into the hole they dig around the grapevine?**
   A. Magical ashes from the *budnik*.
   B. Four pieces of bread.
   C. Three circles of red wine.
   D. All of the above.

Answers: 1-A; 2-C; 3-D; 4-D.

# Spring Rituals

# Orthodox Lenten Season

Spring is a time when nature revives from its winter death. Christians celebrate their greatest holiday, Easter, honoring Christ's death and resurrection after his crucifixion. For many, the season begins with Lent, a period of self-denial, to bring them closer to God.

Lenten holidays have movable dates that depend on when Easter occurs. Most years, the Orthodox Easter falls later than when the Western world celebrates it. This is because the two churches use different calendars. The Western world uses the Gregorian calendar, so the date falls between March 22 and April 25. The Orthodox Church goes by the Julian calendar. When these dates are converted into the Gregorian calendar, Easter occurs between April 4 and May 8.

## ~ PRE-LENTEN HOLIDAYS ~

A few celebrations are sprinkled in before Lent to cleanse the body and soul in preparation for the forty days of fasting prior to Easter. First is All Souls' Day, a time to pay homage to the departed, saying nice things about them so loved ones are remembered. The next day, *Mesni Zagovezni*, or Meat Shrovetide, is the final day before Easter that people can eat meat. The following week, *Sirni Zagovezni*, or Cheese Shrovetide, is the final day people can eat animal byproducts before Easter.

## ~ THE GREAT LENT ~

The forty days of Lent begin the day after *Sirni Zagovezni* and continue until *Lazarovden*, St. Lazarus' Day. Fasting, however, lasts for another week, through Passion Week, and ends on Easter. The days of the first week of Lent have special names and rituals that accompany them.

- The first three days are called *Trimiro*. People of all ages perform an absolute fast (no food or liquid), so they will be forgiven for their sins, but it's done in secret. The fasting is not performed every year, but can be done three, five, seven, or nine years in a row, or three times in one's life.
- Monday is *Kukerovden*, or Mummer's Day, a ritual where men called *kukeri* chase away spirits.
- Black or Bad Tuesday is considered the worst Tuesday of the year.
- Mad Wednesday marks the end of the *Trimiro* fast. Rituals are done to prevent madness.
- On Crazy Thursday, women don't spin wool, in order to avoid getting dizzy or going insane.
- No household work is done on Black Friday, including washing or combing hair. Instead people pay respect to God in prayer.
- The final day of the first week of Lent is *Todorovden*, a day to honor St. Todor. Special celebrations involving horses are also performed.

Eight days before Easter is *Lazarovden*, a day of reverence for St. Lazarus, and also a day of celebration for young girls and unmarried women. This marks the end of the Orthodox Lent.

## ~ PASSION WEEK ~

The week before Easter is called Passion Week, Holy Week, or Great Week. Like the first week of Lent, each day has a special name and rituals associated with it.

- It begins with *Vrabnitsa*, Palm Sunday, also called *Tsvetnitsa*, or Flower Day. This is the day Jesus rode into Jerusalem on a donkey, while people proclaimed him king.
- Cleaning the home begins on Good or Fig Monday. Dancing is forbidden, as well as singing anything except religious songs. Those who disobey risk getting boils all over their bodies.
- On Holy Tuesday, young girls and brides retrieve "silent water" from three locations. Anyone who washes their hair with this water will have health and a long life.

- No housework, sewing, or spinning is done on Holy or Spy Wednesday. This is a day children pick wild geraniums and boil their petals to make red dye to color Easter eggs.
- Easter eggs are dyed on Maudy Thursday, which is also called Sweet or Great Thursday.
- On Good, or Crucified Friday, people refrain from work, so fields won't be cursed and destroyed by hail. Washing is also prohibited, but baking bread and buns with new yeast is acceptable. A household without fresh yeast would remain empty, and the family's crops would be barren.
- Great, or Funeral, Saturday is a day people pay homage to the dead by visiting graveyards. They light candles, burn incense, pour wine onto the grave, and eat meals of bread and boiled wheat mixed with sugar and walnuts as on other All Souls' Days.

All of this culminates into Easter, or Great Day, the greatest rising from death in Christian belief.

*The 2016 calendar below lists some of the spring holidays Bulgarians celebrate.*

**MARCH 2016**

| Sun | Mon | Tue | Wed | Thu | Fri | Sat |
|---|---|---|---|---|---|---|
| | | 1<br>Granny Marta Day<br><br>Baba Marta Den | 2 | 3 | 4 | 5<br>All Souls' Day<br><br>Zadushnitza |
| 6<br>Meat Shrovetide<br><br>Mesni Zagovezni | 7 | 8 | 9 | 10 | 11 | 12 |
| 13<br>Cheese Shrovetide or Forgiveness Sunday<br><br>Sirni Zagovezni | LENT BEGINS 14<br>Clean Monday or Mummers' Day<br><br>Kukerovden | 15<br>Black Tuesday | 16<br>Mad Wednesday | 17<br>Crazy Thursday | 18<br>Black Friday | 19<br>St. Todor's Day or Horse Easter<br><br>Todorovden |
| 20 | 21 | 22 | 23 | 24 | 25<br>Annunciation<br><br>Blagovets | 26 |
| 27 | 28 | 29 | 30 | 31 | | |

**APRIL**

| Sun | Mon | Tue | Wed | Thu | Fri | Sat |
|---|---|---|---|---|---|---|
| | | | | | 1 | 2 |
| 3 | 4 | 5 | 6 | 7 | 8 | 9 |
| 10 | 11 | 12 | 13 | 14 | 15 | 16 |
| 17 | 18 | 19 | 20 | 21 | 22 | 23<br>St. Lazarus' Day<br><br>Lazarovden |
| 24<br>Palm Sunday or Flower Day<br><br>Vrabnitsa or Tsvetnitsa | 25<br>Good (Fig) Monday | 26<br>Holy Tuesday | 27<br>Holy (Spy) Wednesday | 28<br>Sweet (Maudy) Thursday | 29<br>Good (Crucified) Friday | 30<br>Great (Funeral) Saturday |

**MAY**

| Sun | Mon | Tue | Wed | Thu | Fri | Sat |
|---|---|---|---|---|---|---|
| 1<br>Easter<br><br>Velikden | 2 | 3 | 4 | 5 | 6 | 7 |

# Baba Marta Den

**March 1 – Баба Марта Ден – Baba Marta Den: Granny Marta Day.**
**Мартеница – Martenitsa (singular), martenitsi (plural): Little March, amulets worn on this day.**
*The Bulgarian word* Mart *(the feminine of which is* Marta*) means "March." This is the only feminine month of the year. The day is called* letnik*, from* liato*, which means summer. In the ancient world, the year was divided into two seasons, winter and summer, and March 1 ushered in summer.[7] March 1 is the day tradition says corn germinates.*

***Baba Marta Den*** is dedicated to pacifying Baba Marta, an angry old woman who personifies unpredictable March weather that can go from warm and sunny one day to freezing the next. When Marta smiles, she appears as a beautiful young maiden. Her happiness makes the sun shine and spring flowers blossom. When she turns grumpy and frowns, snow and cold winter winds return, and Marta once again becomes a limping, hunchbacked old hag who leans on a stick.

The event that highlights *Baba Marta Den* is making *martenitsi*, amulets of red and white yarn. At one time, the eldest woman in the household made them, then tied them to a rose bush overnight. The next morning, she distributed them to her family after the sun's rays infused the *martenitsi* with magical powers to drive away spirits and disasters. Nowadays, everyone makes them for friends and loved ones.

## Did you know...?

*Older Bulgarians call March "birch month" because leaves on birch trees begin to regrow at this time.*

On her special day, Baba Marta has a tendency to be quite demanding. She expects everyone to honor her by putting on something red, her favorite color, and by wearing a *martenitsa*. She becomes angry and sends bad luck to those who fail to wear the amulet. But, she's displeased if people wear a *martenitsa* they made themselves. This grouchy woman requires everyone to give the amulets to friends and relatives, wishing them health and happiness throughout the year.

## ~ ORIGINS ~

The tradition of wearing *martenitsi* dates back to Thracian times to welcome spring. Orpheus himself supposedly decorated his harp with one.

In times before Bulgaria was Christianized, the *martenitsi* colors represented elements in nature. Red was symbolic of the sun's rays, painting the sky as it rose and set. White was the purity of snow, the last traces melting with winter's retreat. The two tassels twisted together contained magic protection from

---

[7] Panayotova, Rumyana and Konstantinova, Daniela (trans.), "March 1, Granny Martha rites," Feb. 26, 2010, http://bnr.bg/en/post/100103127/march-1-granny-martha-rites.

forces released on the solstice. People even put *martenitsi* on their cattle to make sure the animals remained healthy and fertile.

The name "March" comes from Mars, the god of war and protector of agriculture, whom the Thracians worshipped. Legends claim these people were descended from the god, who was born in Thrace. Thracians were fearsome warriors who hired themselves as mercenaries once snow melted in March, and they could travel to foreign lands. As men prepared to leave, women made *martenitsi* charms from red and white strips of cloth, then wrapped them around the men's hands to protect them in battle. Red signified blood spilled during war, and white represented the paleness of women's faces as their men headed off to fight. The charms were also meant to appease Baba Marta. By displaying this color, women hoped Marta would keep the weather warm and free of storms so soldiers wouldn't die from the cold.

After Bulgaria adopted Christianity, the colors represented their new religious beliefs. Red was symbolic of virginity and virtue, as well as protection from illness. White denoted Christ and long life. Together, they embodied the blood shed for new life. Additionally, in one story, the Virgin Mary dyed a strip of a white skirt in her blood, then tore off another piece and twisted the two together. She wrapped them across her body, went outside as the sun rose, and announced a blessing on her fertility.

## ~ RITUALS IN PRACTICE ~

On the final evening of February, the Pavlovs sit in the kitchen. Red and white yarn, beads, coins, scissors, and cardboard litter the table. Maria helps Niki twist a strand of red yarn with a white one.

Rada's completed a boy charm, Pijo, and now she's finishing the girl. She holds the female up for her mother's inspection. "Here's Penda." The red charm sways at one end of the twisted thread, while the boy, made with white yarn, lies on the table attached to the other end. "I only have to trim the bottom."

"Lovely," Maria says. "You've perfected the art."

Niki shows his sister his. "How do you like mine?"

"Nice," she says. "Your strands are twisted evenly."

"I want Baba to wear mine."

Rada hands him a blue eye bead. "Add this and a coin. They protect against harm and illness."

"Really?" Niki looks from Rada to his mother.

"Yes," Maria says. "Your sister's telling you the truth. Baba will be glad you want to protect her."

When they finish, Niki sighs. "I wish Baba was awake. I want to hear a story about *martenitsi*."

"I remember some she's told," Rada says. "How about I tell you one about Penda and Pijo?" She holds the middle of the twisted string, and the dolls dance in the air.

"You will?"

"Sure, I want to practice on someone. Let's sit on the couch."

**Penda and Pijo**

"A long time ago," Rada begins, "a Tsar named Pijo loved a woman named Penda."

Niki puts his hands on his forehead. "Not a *love* story!"

"Stop it." She removes his hands. "You'll like this one. It has a soldier and fighting."

"Okay, but no kissing. Yuck." Niki wipes his mouth.

Rada laughs. "Don't worry. There isn't any kissing."

"Good. Tell me about the soldier."

"Penda was kidnapped by a bad man who lived far away," Rada says. "When Pijo found out, he wanted to search for her, but he couldn't leave his kingdom."

Niki leans closer. "How's he going to find her then?"

27

"The Tsar sent carrier pigeons with messages asking his loyal subjects if they'd seen Penda. He also asked a brave, trusted soldier to look for her. He left on a hot summer day, and searched well into winter."

"That's a long time. I hope the soldier brought a warm jacket so he didn't freeze."

"I'm sure he did," Rada says. "Far from his homeland, he met an old woman and eleven old men sitting on the cold ground by a well. The old woman struggled to rise, so the soldier helped her, then lifted the bucket of water from the well to give her a drink."

"That was nice of him," Niki says.

"Yes, it was. The woman thought so, too. She said, 'I'm Baba Marta—' "

"Oh no! Did she send a blizzard to freeze the soldier?"

"No, silly. Let me finish the story. I'll get to the fighting soon."

"Okay." Niki clasps his hands and sits still.

"The old woman told him the men were her brothers, the other eleven months of the year. 'Because you've been kind to me,' she said, 'you'll find what you're looking for.' "

"What was he looking for?" Niki asks.

"Don't you remember? Penda."

"Oh, yah."

"Soon the soldier discovered the house where Penda was held prisoner. He untied her and was going to take her home, when the man who kidnapped her returned."

Niki slashes his hands through the air as if wielding a sword. "Now they're going to fight?"

"Yes, they fought for many hours. The soldier tired and feared his strength would fail. He jabbed once more and killed the bad man, then collapsed. Penda gave him a drink of water. 'Our journey back will take a long time,' she said. 'I must let Pijo know I'm safe.' She wrote a note and placed it inside a tube. With a white thread, she tied it to the leg of a carrier pigeon Pijo had sent, then released the bird."

### Did you know...?

*Many birds fly over Bulgaria when they migrate. It has one of the highest bird concentrations in Europe: 397 recorded species.*

"How would the bird find Pijo?" Niki asks.

"Carrier pigeons are smart. They know how to find their way home."

"Did the bird make it back?"

"Yes, but it scraped its leg on a branch. Blood stained the thread."

"I hope it didn't mess up what she wrote, or Pijo wouldn't know she was okay," Niki says.

"The message was fine. When Pijo read it, he was so happy. He tied the blood-stained thread to his shirt until Penda returned safely. That's one story about why we use red and white to make *martenitsi*."

Niki twists in his seat to look at Rada. "You know another one?"

"Yes, one about Asparuh and Huba, a brother and sister."

"Oh, tell me that one, please!"

**Asparauh and Huba**

Rada smiles. "This story takes place on March 1, 681, when the first Bulgarian Empire was established. Khan Asparuh of the Bulgars looked for a safe place to live after the Huns invaded. He discovered a new land south of the Danube River. He sent a falcon with a message to his sister Huba."

"Where was she? Why wasn't she with him?"

"The Huns had her locked in a prison."

"I want to hear about the Huns fighting."

"I'm sure Baba can tell you that some other time. Right now, I want to tell you how the *martenitsa* tradition began." Rada taps her fingers on her leg. "Now, may I continue? I think you'll like this one."

"Sure." Niki sits back into the cushion.

"King Asparuh sent a falcon to his sister. It carried a message that he had found a new homeland. If she could escape, the falcon would lead her there."

"Not a carrier pigeon?" Niki asks.

"Nope, a falcon in this story. Anyway, Huba escaped and fled on horseback, following the falcon to the Danube. But the river was flooded. She didn't know where to cross safely, but then she got an idea."

"What?" Niki leans closer.

"She waited until the falcon came down to rest. Then she tied a long, white thread to its leg. When it flew up high, it looked for a safe passage. It found one and glided to the other side of the river. Huba hurried after the falcon. But then ..." Rada pauses, closing her eyes.

"Well? What happened?" Niki's voice escalates. "Tell me, quick!"

Rada opens her eyes and leans forward. "The bird spun and fell to the ground like a rocket. Huba looked behind her. An enemy soldier had pierced the falcon with an arrow."

"Is she going to get away?"

Rada smiles, then lowers her voice. "Huba galloped the horse through a shallow spot in the river. She snatched up the falcon, his blood streaming down the thread. It had saved her, and she wanted to give it a decent burial. She managed to escape her pursuers, to be reunited with her brother."

"I bet he was angry his falcon was dead."

"I'm sure he did miss his bird," Rada says. "But he was thankful his sister arrived safely. He removed the blood-stained thread from the falcon's leg, cut it, and tied the pieces to his soldiers' hands, commanding them to never separate the red and white so their new land would remain safe and unified." She swings her *martenitsa* in front of Niki's face. "That's how we started making these good-luck charms."

"You should have told me that story instead of the yucky love story. It was way better."

"You might like another version even more, then. It doesn't have a happy ending."

"Tell me, please!"

# How to Wear *Martenitsi*

*Most often, people wear the amulet on clothing, or around their neck or wrist. Traditionally, children wear one on their right wrist or as a necklace. The placement on women's clothing indicates their marital status. Married women wear a* martenitsa *on the right, while single women place it on the left. Unmarried or newly married women often wear one around their neck or woven into their hair. Elderly people tend to keep the* martenitsa *orderly. Bachelors, on the other hand, spread out the threads. Men also may wear one on their waistband, or on the left, either on their pinky, elbow, or unseen on their ankle, or even in their shoe beneath their heel. Wearing the amulet on their wrist could indicate that their masculinity was "tied up" by a woman.*

"In this one, the Huns held Huba and another brother, Bayan, prisoners. They both escaped, but were wounded. When they stumbled across the Danube, Asparuh tried to save them, but they died in his arms. He ordered his soldiers to wear the blood-stained thread in remembrance of his siblings' bravery."

"That's awesome!" Niki gets off the couch and staggers around the room, finally dropping to the ground clutching his chest. He looks back at Rada. "Do you know any more?"

Rada purses her lips. "There's one with a swallow. In that one the Khan's sister is Khalina, and she's not a prisoner, but far away in the mountains of Tibet. Khan Asparuh traveled to the place that's now Bulgaria, where he met women dressed in white—"

Niki sits up quickly. "*Samodivi*?"

"I don't think so. They fed him a great feast instead of harming him," Rada says. "One day, a swallow sat on the Khan's shoulder. He told the bird how he longed to see his family. What he didn't know was the bird understood him. It flew to his sister, repeating how he missed her. Khalina decided to go live with him. She tied a bouquet of flowers to the bird's foot with a white thread, then sent it to her brother."

"Is this one going to get shot with an arrow?" Niki asks.

"No, but the bird did hurt its wing when it stopped to rest on a tree. The blood trickled down as it flew and coated the thread, so it was red by the time the bird reached the Khan. He attached the thread to his clothing over his heart."

"Oh, so that's why some people wear the *martenitsa* as a pin instead of on their wrists," Niki says, then covers his mouth, laughing. "I'm sure the flowers must have been dead by the time the bird arrived."

Rada laughs with him. "Probably. I think another version says his sister sent him a sprig of dill, instead of a bouquet of flowers. The Khan started a fire with it since he was preparing an offering to the god Tangra. He wore the thread as a charm to ensure his health."

Niki looks around, then returns to the couch. "The last one sounds like something Mom would do."

"You're right. Well, that's all the stories I know about the *martenitsa*."

## Marta's Mood

Baba claps her hands. "Well done. You're a natural story teller."

"Baba!" Niki gets up and hugs her. "Will you tell me another story?"

"I think you've had enough stories today." Baba sits in her rocker. "Right now your mother, sister, and I want to predict Marta's mood."

"She always seems grumpy to me." Niki frowns and heads to his room.

Maria sits next to Rada. "My little boy is the grumpy one when he doesn't get his fill of stories."

"It was fun telling him about *martenitsi*," Rada replies, "but now it's time for adult matters. I hope I pick a day when Marta's in a good mood and sends us warm weather. I'd hate to be stuck like Helena with a cold, wet, miserable day. She was cranky all year." She turns to her grandmother. "Baba, what day do you choose?"

Baba puts her hand on her chin and thinks. "I say Marta will be happy on March 15, so I can be happy and successful all year."

"Mom, how about you? What's your day?"

"I'm going to pick tomorrow, March 1. I haven't heard any bad forecasts. Now, it's your turn, Rada."

"I pick March 22. It'll officially be spring, and the weather should be warm and sunny by then."

## Clean and Red

The next morning, a few hours before dawn, everyone, including Niki, is awake. They cross themselves three times, then begin the task of cleaning to appease Marta. Maria and Rada tackle the kitchen, which is on the eastern side of the house. They make their way from room to room. First east to west, then north to south, in the shape of a cross.

When they get to Baba's room, the elderly woman retreats to the comfort of her rocker. Niki follows, "Baba Marta! Today is your day. Happy *Baba Marta Den.*"

Rada motions to him as he's about to sit near his grandmother. "You can finish tidying up your room, Niki. We have too much else to clean and can't pick up after you."

He sulks. "I wanted Baba to tell me a story."

"Do as your sister asks," Baba tells him. "I'll tell you a story later."

"Why do we have to do so much cleaning today?" Niki mumbles as he shuffles off.

"We don't want to make the first Baba Marta angry on her day," Rada replies. "We have to meet her 'clean and red.' Last night we made the *martenitsi.* Today we'll wear red because she likes that color, and we have to clean so our house is as immaculate as Baba Marta's."

"What does it matter if she gets mad anyway?"

"When she's irritable, she sends us bad weather. You'd like to be able to play outside more with your friends, wouldn't you?"

"Yah. But why should she care if *my* room is messy?"

"Maybe because she had to pick up after a lazy brother, too." Rada says. "I'll let you beat the *cherga* outside this year if you hurry and clean your room."

"The red one?" He glances at the runner in the hallway. Decorating its border are geometric shapes symbolizing the World Tree and other shapes representing spring and fertility.

"Yes. Red puts her in a good mood so she laughs and makes the day sunny. We need a lot of sun so crops grow healthy and high."

Niki dashes to his room, tosses everything lying on the floor into a toy box, picks up dirty clothes and puts them into the laundry basket, then grabs his wooden club. "I'm done."

He drags the rug outside. Balkan runs out the open door. Niki drapes the rug over the fence and hits it with his club. Dust flies all around, and he sneezes. When he tires, he sits on the ground. He peeks under the rose bush. "Look, Balkan. The *martenitsi* Baba put here last night."

Georgi walks onto the porch and hangs a red cloth under the eaves. Balkan runs over to him, barking.

"Dad," Niki says, "can I bring the *martenitsi* to Baba? See the sun is shining on them now."

"I'm sure she'd appreciate that."

Niki snatches the bowl and runs into the house. "Baba, wear the *martenitsa* I made. Please!"

"Of course."

He hands her the container and picks up the charm with a blue bead and coin woven into it.

"You added everything but garlic to prevent hardship."

"Rada told me those would protect you from getting sick, and the red would keep bad things away."

"She's right," Baba says. "Thank you. In my village, we added a blue thread to ward off the evil eye."

"I'll make you one like that next year."

"Will you tell everyone I'm ready?" Baba looks over the gift. "And ask your mother for a pin?"

The family gathers around Baba, and she gives each person an amulet they didn't make. "It's bad luck to wear your own *martenitsa*," she says. She pins hers to her apron and straightens the threads. "Now I'm ready to tell you stories about Baba Marta."

"Yeah!" Niki claps his hands. "Baba Marta's gonna tell us about Baba Marta."

## Baba Marta and Stolen Wine

"Baba Marta lived with her two brothers. Goliam, or 'Big Month,' Sechko was in charge of January, and Malak, or 'Little Month,' Sechko took care of February. The three of them lived high in the mountains in a large, beautiful mansion." Baba rocks her chair. "Because she appreciated lovely things, Marta made sure her home was always clean, and everything was where it belonged."

Rada gives Niki a look that says, "See, I told you."

"Marta and her brothers worked long hours in their thriving vineyards," Baba continues. "They produced a lot of excellent wine every year."

"Just like Dad," Niki says.

"Yes, that's true," Baba replies. "During the winter, they liked to constantly drink wine they made the previous year."

Niki snickers. "Like Dad on *Trifonovden*."

"Shh." Rada looks around, but her father isn't nearby.

Baba only smiles. "Marta was not like her brothers. She preferred to save her wine for special occasions, like her own day, today."

"I bet she made red wine since that's her favorite color," Niki says.

"I'm sure you're right," Baba agrees. "One year after they had made a lot of exceptional wine, Marta climbed down the steps to the basement where they stored the casks."

"Did she have to use her cane?" Rada prompts when Baba hesitates.

"No. She was happy because it was her day to celebrate, so she was young, beautiful, healthy, and had a spring in her step."

"Just like Rada." Niki grins. "Especially when boys are nearby."

"Hush!" Rada glares at him. "Let Baba tell the story." She turns back to look at her grandmother. "Did she pick out a Thracian wine?"

"Unfortunately, when she looked, all her wine casks were empty." Baba sighs, as if she has made the discovery herself. "She checked her brothers' casks, too." Baba pauses. "*All* of them were empty."

Niki gasps. "Someone stole the wine!"

"Yes," Baba says. "Marta was sure it was her brothers who drank it. She limped upstairs, breathing hard by the time she reached the top. Her anger made her hunchbacked and old."

"Poor Marta." Rada looks at her grandmother who has been having trouble walking.

"Indeed," Baba agrees. "But it was more than Marta who suffered. She was so furious, she punished the land with winter storms much of the month of March."

Niki peeks out the window, where it's sunny. "I guess her brothers didn't steal her wine today."

"Marta finally forgave her brothers after they promised to never do that again," Baba says. "They even gave her some of the wine they made the next year, making her smile again. As soon as she did, the warm weather returned and melted the snow. Trees budded, flowers bloomed, and spring filled the land."

## Baba Marta and Borrowed Days

"Baba, please tell me another story about Marta." Niki looks at her with eyes as round as Balkan's.

"One more. Then you have to go outside to help your father clean the yard," Baba says. "Marta expects outside to be as tidy as inside."

"Tell the one about the woman and the goats," Rada says.

"That's a good one. Yes, I'll tell you that." Her voice cracks.

"Maybe we should let Baba rest, Niki." Rada gets up, pours a glass of water, and hands it to Baba.

"Thank you, dear. It's a short story. I'll rest after this one." Baba takes a long drink, then clears her throat. "I told you how Marta likes beautiful things. Seeing young, beautiful people puts her in a good mood, but she gets angry if old people go outside today."

"She'd like you." Niki leans forward and holds Baba's hand.

"Maybe," Baba says, "but another old woman thought Marta would like her, too, since Marta herself was often an old woman, but that woman was wrong."

"What did Marta do?" Niki tightens his grip on his grandmother's hand.

"You'll see," Baba says. "Long ago, February had thirty-one days, the same as January, and March had only twenty-eight. Three days before February ended, an old woman wanted to take her goats to graze in a meadow because the weather was nice. 'Marta, can't hurt me today,' the woman thought. 'Even if it was her month, I'm sure she'd have compassion on another old woman and bless me with good weather.' When Marta saw the woman outside, she fumed."

"Oh no," Niki says. "Did she send snow?"

"It was her brother's month, so Marta couldn't change the weather. This made her even more angry."

"Good." Niki loosens his grip a little. "She can't hurt the old woman."

"Marta stomped into Little Sechko's room and demanded he give her three days in exchange for the wine he had stolen," Baba replies. "He did, so now, instead of it being February, it was March, and Marta could control the weather."

"Didn't he already give her extra wine?" Niki asks.

"Yes, but she insisted he do as she told him. She sent a terrible blizzard for those three days. The woman and her goats froze and turned into a pile of stones."

Niki frowns. "Marta's mean. That poor woman. What if she does that to you?"

"Don't worry," Baba says. "I won't go outside on Marta's day."

"It's not all bad," Rada adds. "When the snow melted, it formed a river coming out of the stones. The water had healing power, and people often went there to visit the spot, and they said nice things about the woman."

## Purifying Fires

Rada rises and looks out the window. "Dad's raking up the yard, and Mom's helping him. He already has the fire going. Why don't you go join them, Niki? I'll collect the trash inside and bring it out."

"Okay." Niki kisses Baba. "Make sure you stay inside. I don't want Marta to hurt you."

She touches the *martenitsa* Niki made for her. "This will protect me."

"Good." Niki looks at the blue bead, then walks toward the door.

"Wait, Niki." Rada stops him. "First put on a red scarf. Marta wants to see lots of red today. The more we show her, the nicer the month will be."

"And don't leave white clothes outside," Baba adds. "That'll make Marta send hailstorms and frost."

"Okay." Niki puts on gloves, wraps the scarf around his neck, and rushes outside. Balkan squeezes out the door and chases leaves stirred up by Georgi's and Maria's raking. Niki asks his father, "What can I do?"

Georgi hands him a small basket. "You can put leaves and twigs in here, then dump them on the fire. But be careful not to get too close to the flames."

"Yup." Niki places the basket on the ground and pushes leaves into it. When it's full, he drags it to the fire and dumps the debris. The fire crackles and sparks fly.

Rada, wearing a red jacket, tosses old papers onto the fire. As soon as the yard is clear, the family waits for the flames to die down.

"Who wants to jump over the fire first?" Georgi asks.

"Me, me, me!" Niki runs around.

"Okay. Face the sun," Georgi says. "Stay on the side, and not the middle."

Niki chooses a spot with mostly coals. He squints at the sun, then back at the fire.

Rada holds onto Balkan so he doesn't follow Niki.

"Now jump over the fire three times from that spot," Georgi says. "Ready ... go."

Niki backs up, runs, and jumps over the fire. He laughs and does it again, and then a third time. Rada goes next.

Niki says to his father, "That was fun. I wish we did that every day."

"We'll have more holidays where we'll jump over fire. Do you know why we do this?"

"Because Marta doesn't like messes," Niki says.

Georgi grins. "Yes, that, and Baba would tell you it warms Marta. A long time ago, even before our Baba was born, people thought if they were good to Marta, she'd return the favor and not let the sun get too hot while they worked in the fields."

Niki shivers. "It's not too hot now."

"Not yet," Georgi agrees. "Your mother says fire protects us from illness and gets rid of gremlins hiding in the litter and dark places around the house. The same as when she burns incense."

"We seem to have a lot of those pests." Niki says. "Baba and Mom keep doing all kinds of things to get rid of them."

Georgi bends down and whispers, "I think they have fun doing it. And they don't like snakes and lizards. The fires help keep them away, too."

## Signs of Spring

"You're right, I don't like snakes." Maria joins her husband and son.

"Mom, I love the *martenitsa* you made." He twirls the amulet around his wrist. A bead with an *N* catches the sunlight. "I want to wear it forever."

"You can wear it until spring officially arrives anyway."

"When's that?"

"Some people keep it on until *Blagovets* on March 25," Maria says. "Others take it off on March 9."

"My favorite way to tell spring is here," Georgi says, "is when you see a stork flying."

### Did you know...?

*Snow at the end of winter that falls in large flakes is called "stork's snow" because it means birds are beginning their return migration.*

"Why?" Niki asks.

"It means you'll be 'flying high' yourself."

"What does that mean?"

"Everything's going to be great," Georgi says. "When I was a boy, I saw an entire flock of storks flying back in the spring. I threw my amulet up toward them and shouted, 'Here is a gift for you, my *martenitsa*. Please give me health and prosperity.' Some of my friends saw storks after they had landed. They were happy about that."

"Why?" Niki asks.

"It meant their summer was going to be lazy and carefree." Georgi pauses. "They played all summer while I worked. But I had money to spend."

"I want to see a stork flying," Niki says. "I'd like to have money to buy things."

"I'm sure I can use a hand in the vineyard this summer." Georgi smiles at his son. "You can also look for a few other things to tell it's spring."

"What?"

"Sparrow, cuckoos, or ..." He winks at Maria. "You can try to find a snake sunning itself on a rock."

Rada comes over. "Baba says you can even throw your *martenitsa* into a river. All your troubles will float away like the leaves that fall there. Then the year will be trouble-free."

# Try This: *Martenitsa* Predictions

When spring arrives, place your martenitsa *under a stone. Check it nine days later. If the tassels are covered with a lot of bugs, fields will be fertile for farming. The type of insect found makes the prediction vary.*

- **Beetles** *indicate a healthy, successful year.*
- *If the bracelet is mostly covered with **ants**, you'll be successful if you work hard. It also means sheep will produce many young.*
- *If **ladybugs** and other larger bugs are all around the* martenitsa, *cattle will be plentiful.*
- **Worms** *indicate the birth of many horses.*
- *On the negative side, finding a **snake** is bad luck, and a **spider** indicates ill health and lack of success.*

# Making Penda and Pijo Martenitsi

White wool yarn or silk
Red wool yarn or silk
Small piece of cardboard, 3x3 inches

Pair of scissors
Glue gun (optional)
Plastic doll eyes (optional)

A *martenitsa* symbolizes good wishes to those you give them to. In order to make a *martenitsa*, you need white and red wool yarn and a lot of imagination. Have fun!

**Create Twisted Braid**
➤ Cut off about 12 - 24 inches from both the red and white yarn.
➤ Tie the two together in a knot.
➤ Secure one end of the yarn with a safety pin to something that will not move.
➤ Hold the other end of the yarn and twist it until it is tight.
➤ With one hand still holding the yarn at the end you twisted, grasp the place where you tied them together.
➤ Release the end that you twisted to let the two strands wrap around each other.
➤ Smooth out as necessary so the two strands are uniformly entwined.

**Make Pompoms**
➤ Wind red yarn one way around the cardboard 10 - 15 times.
➤ Insert the twisted braid under all the strands at one end.
➤ Pull the braid tight together to compress the strands, and then tie the braid together with another piece of red yarn.
➤ Cut the red threads at the bottom of the opposite end of the cardboard, and remove the cardboard.
➤ Repeat the above process with white thread, using the other end of the twisted braid.

*Continues on next page.*

# Making Penda and Pijo Martenitsi

**Make *Penda***

> **Doll's Head:** Tie a red thread on the red pompom about 1/2 inch below the place where it is attached to the braid. The strand of yarn should be long enough so that each end reaches to the bottom of the pompom to blend in with the others.
> **Waist:** Pull out a few strands on each side of the pompom to use for the hands.
> Wrap a strand of white yarn a few times around the remaining pompom about 1 1/2 inches from the top where it is attached to the thread, pulling it tight.
> Tie the yarn into a bow, or weave the ends into the inside of the "belt" to hide them.
> Cut off any excess yarn.
> **Arms:** Twist a piece of red yarn around the strands left for one of the arms about 1 1/2 inches out from the body.
> Tie it tight and cut the excess yarn. Weave it in if you can.
> Repeat for the other arm.

**Make *Pijo***

> Repeat the above steps for the head, waist, and arms, using the opposite colors: white to tie head and arms, but red for the waist.
> **Legs:** Cut the bottom of the pompom so the stands are equal.
> Separate the threads into two equal parts.
> Twist a piece of white yarn around one leg about 1/4 inch from the bottom.
> Tie it tight and cut the excess yarn. Weave it in if you can.
> Repeat for the other leg.

**Add Eyes**

> You can now add eyes if you want or leave the *martenitsi* as they are.
> Attach two eyes to each doll with a glue gun.

*Martenitsi* are decorated in various ways in different parts of Bulgaria. In southern Bulgaria, instead of white thread, people weave in a blue thread (to guard against the evil eye). In the Rhodope Mountains, people use a few more colors. Remember, *martenitsi* are given to others to wear on March 1 as a token of friendship. Make sure you don't wear the one you made.

# Sirni Zagovezni

**\*March 13 – Сирни Заговезни – Sirni Zagovezni: Cheese Shrovetide, Shrove Sunday, Forgiveness Sunday.**
Sunday, the day before Lent begins, seven weeks before Easter.
*The holiday gets its name from the fact that this is the final day before Easter on which people can eat any animal byproducts, including cheese.*
*\*A moveable holiday that depends on when Easter is celebrated.*

Bulgarians participate in more than one hundred fast days throughout the year. ***Sirni Zagovezni*** and *Mesni Zagovezni*, are two that occur immediately before the forty days of fasting during the Great Lent. *Mesni Zagovezni* is the final day people are allowed to eat meat before Easter, and *Sirni Zagovezni* is the last day they can consume items produced from animals, things such as eggs, butter, and milk. On these two holidays, the meals are filled with dishes made from these items.

*Sirni Zagovezni* is also a day the Orthodox Church has set aside to ask for forgiveness—first from God, then from older people. This act is meant to bring peace and a sense of new beginnings to those seeking forgiveness.

The day has a less serious side, too. Children play a game where they attempt to catch a sweet with their teeth, while keeping their hands behind their backs. In the evening, young people perform various fire games and participate in a wild *horo* dance one final time before the somberness and restrictions of Lent begin the following day. From this day until Lent, even marriages cannot take place.

## Did you know...?

*If a person dies during the* Trimiro *fast (the first three days of Lent), he's considered a sinner too great to have his sins forgiven. Such a person won't be buried in a graveyard and will become a vampire if he doesn't have a cornel stake driven through his heart.*

## ~ ORIGINS ~

If you recall, pagan spring rituals represent the cycle of birth, death, and resurrection. People in antiquity believed that at each equinox when the seasons changed, spirits entered man's world and brought chaos. Even today, people allege that on All Souls' Day spirits of the dead return to the world and remain until Pentecost, fifty days after Easter.

### Fertility

This festivity originates from celebrations of the New Moon in ancient times. Much like the winter solstice celebrated the birth of the new sun, spring rites were associated with fertility, the waxing (growing) moon. Thracians celebrated them in honor of Bendis, the Great Goddess of the moon and the hunt, often associated with the Greek goddess Artemis.

The celebrations also have a connection to the sun. Children swing torches to drive spirits away. Since fire is related to the sun, building bonfires is believed to revive that heavenly fire, and also encourage the soil to produce more wheat.

**Fasting**

In an attempt to return order to the world when spirits crossed the realms, people in antiquity fasted. Before they did this, however, they held wild, perverse rituals.

The denial and restrictions of fasting provided them a way to open their minds to the gods. By fasting, a person figuratively died and was born again, like the rebirth of nature after winter, and the death and resurrection of their gods. It was a way to purify body and spirit, returning harmony between physical man and spiritual nature. Breaking the fast returned the world to a state of chaos.[8]

How did these practices make their way into Christianity? In order to bring pagans to accept one god, the early Church leaders adopted many pagan symbols and rituals. For example, the worshipers of pagan gods fasted from meat for forty days as a time of mourning and sorrow. For the Church this became a representation of Christ fasting forty days in the desert before he entered his ministry.

**Forgiveness**

The Day of Atonement, Yom Kippur, is part of the Hebrew heritage Christianity started from. It was the only day when the High Priest could enter the most sacred room in the temple, the Holy of Holies. It was here he offered a blood sacrifice for the sins of the nation. When people confessed their sins, cleansing their souls, it was as if they could figuratively stand in the presence of God in the temple along with the High Priest.

## ~ RITUALS IN PRACTICE ~

Early in the morning on *Sirni Zagovezni*, the Pavlov family begins the preparations for the festivities.

Niki, with Balkan trailing behind, comes bounding into the kitchen. "Mom, we better hurry. The sun's coming up. We want to go to the *horo* dance in the village."

Maria places a *banitsa* into the oven. "Today the *horo* will be at sunset."

"Oh, I wanted to see Yordan." He dips his finger into the bowl with the leftover batter, then licks it. "We're not having *banitsa* with ham today?"

"No, Niki," Baba says as she finishes making *katmi*. "No more meat until Easter. Today, we'll have lots of food with eggs, cheese, and butter because we'll be fasting from those, too."

"No more *banitsa* until Easter?" He sets the bowl on the floor for Balkan to lick.

"Niki!" Rada snatches it and rinses it. "That's not for the dog to eat."

Niki moans. "What are we going to be able to eat until Easter if we can't have meat or cheese or—"

"Niki." His mother lowers her face to him and frowns. "None of that."

"Come and sit with me." Baba piles a plate with *katmi* and sets it on the table. "What would you like on yours?"

"Honey!"

He scoots into the chair next to his grandmother and takes one of the thin pancakes from the stack, pours melted butter over it, then drips honey on top. He adds two more, layering them like a cake.

Baba puts her hand out as he reaches for one more. "I think three's enough for now."

---

[8] Nikov, Nikola, "ZADOUSHNITZA (All Souls' Day)," from "Holidays of the Bulgarians in Myths and Legends," http://www.promacedonia.org/bg_folklore/en/index.htm.

# Dance the *Horo*

*The* horo, *performed in a circle, is the most popular dance in Bulgaria and is part of all major rituals. The performers link hands low at their sides. As they dance, they shout and jump. Their feet often move quickly in intricate patterns, but the steps can also be slow and elegant. Not only is the* horo *fun to watch and participate in, but it has a spiritual side, connecting dancers with the world around them. This concept possibly comes from the Thracians. Dancing enabled them to synchronize with the rhythm of nature and absorb its energy. In the past, a man played the* gaida *from within the middle of the circle, while dancers moved in a counterclockwise direction around him. To the ancient people, this would be how they saw the sun move in the sky, from east to west, around Earth. Likewise, joining hands demonstrated the unity of the community.*

## Bonfire

Georgi enters the room and loads his plate with *katmi*. "Niki, when we're done eating, do you want to help me collect leaves and twigs for the bonfire tonight?"

"Yes, please." Niki shovels his food in.

"Slow down." Georgi puts his hand on his son's arm. "We'll go after the sun comes up so we can see what we're putting into the *kosh*."

After breakfast, Niki walks to the shed with his father and tugs at the basket made from willow branches. "Can I carry it?"

"You're a bit too small for that. The basket's almost as tall as you are." Georgi loads the basket, rakes, and a hatchet onto a cart. "You can help me push this if you want."

They rake leaves and stuff them into the basket.

"Let's have our bonfire on the hill behind our house." Georgi points. "See? I already started a pile with branches from the tree I cut for the *budnik*."

"We'll have to make it really big so ours is the tallest," Niki says. "I want to win."

"That's not quite what the bonfire is about." Georgi pushes the cart up the hill. "We want the flames to shoot high into the sky so they light up as much of our property as possible."

"Why?" Niki stops walking to scratch Balkan behind the ears.

"Wherever light touches will be safe from hail in the summer." At the top of the hill, Georgi dumps the leaves over the branches. "When we're done here, we can help build the bonfire in the village center."

## Asking Forgiveness

Tired from so much work, Niki falls asleep after lunch. Rada wakes him a couple of hours later. "Wake up, sleepyhead. It's time to ask forgiveness."

"What did I do?" He rubs his eyes and peers at his sister.

"This is 'Forgiveness Sunday.' Remember?"

"Um, yeah." Niki slips out of bed and puts his shoes on. "Why do we ask forgiveness from Baba?"

"It's to make us pure before we start Lent. We fast and ask for forgiveness before we celebrate the resurrection on Easter."

In the living room, Rada takes Baba's hand, touches it to her forehead, kisses it, then touches her forehead again. "Forgive me," she says.

Baba smiles. "I give you forgiveness, and may the Lord give you forgiveness, as well."

Rada nudges the still-yawning Niki forward. "Your turn."

He repeats the ceremony, then kisses Baba on both cheeks. "Do we get to play *hamkane* now? I've waited a *whole* year for this."

"After we eat supper," his mother says, emerging from the kitchen. "You can invite Yordan and your other friends for dinner and the game. It's more fun if there are more than two." She looks at Rada. "That is, if you sister still wants to play."

"Not this year," Rada says in a matter-of-fact tone. "I'm not a child any longer."

**Child's Play**

Soon the house is full of noisy youngsters. Maria lights incense and spreads the smoke around the table before they eat a light supper of *banitsa*, boiled eggs, halva with walnuts, and rice and milk. After the meal, the children run to the living room and sit on the floor in a semicircle around Baba. She ties one end of a strand of red yarn around a chunk of white halva, and the other end around the tip of a long, thin rolling pin. "Everybody put your hands behind your backs," she tells the children.

When they do, she holds the other end of the rolling pin and swings the sweet in a circle. Each child leans forward, trying to catch it with his teeth as it passes by. They laugh, gasp, and groan as they miss.

Maria nudges Rada. "Are you sure you don't want to join them?"

"I'm positive."

"When I was a child, my baba twirled three strings: coal, a hardboiled egg, and a piece of cheese."

Rada grimaces. "Ugh, coal. Who'd want to catch that, especially with their teeth?"

"It wasn't tasty, but if you caught it, you'd be the one to take care of the home." Maria nudges her daughter. "Some of us girls wanted to have our own homes back then."

"Not me. I want to go to college and see the world," Rada says. "What did the egg and cheese mean? I'd rather catch them."

"Catching the egg meant you'd be lucky, and the cheese, a long life."

"How did your baba swing three at once? It seems hard enough to do one," Rada says.

"My dayado tied the strands of yarn to a nail on the ceiling beam, then twirled them around. It was crazy with kids trying to catch them."

A shriek makes them jump. They turn to see Yordan with his mouth clamped onto the halva.

"Uh whon!" He removes his hands from behind his back and takes the sweet out. "I won! I'm going to be lucky all year."

"Congratulations, Yordan," everyone shouts from around the room.

Baba removes the thread from the rolling pin and tosses it into the fireplace. As it twists around, she proclaims, "The grape harvest will be plentiful again this year."

Niki steps close to look at the blackening yarn. "How can you tell from that?"

"Some secrets are meant to be kept." She smiles. "I'll tell your mother one day, or maybe Rada."

**Fire Games**

Georgi says, "I'm going to start our bonfire, then we can go watch the *horo* and fire games."

"I want to spin the *oratnika* this year!" Niki shouts.

"You can. You're old enough. I'll help you and the other boys make them when I get back."

"Yeah!" Niki twirls around. "Spin the *oratnika*!"

The other boys chant with him. Rada covers her ears. "We can't get them out of here soon enough."

When Georgi returns, the boys gather around, continuing to chant, "Spin the *oratnika*!"

"Yes, yes." Georgi holds the door open. "Come with me and give the women some peace."

Georgi leads them to a pile of sticks and straw. "Everyone take a stick and split it on the end. Then attach straw in the groove. We'll light them from the bonfire when we get to the village." Georgi glances up as Maria, Rada, and Baba emerge from the house, ready to leave. "Let's go, boys."

In addition to the bonfire, several small fires burn in the village. Young men jump over them for good health and protection from snakes and misfortune. They cheer for one another, and toss out playful jests. "You jumped the farthest, Pavel. You're going to get married this autumn. Who's the unlucky girl?"

Niki raps his father on the back with his stick. "Can we light them now, please?"

"Leave the tapping for *Survaki*," Georgi says. "But, yes, come with me. All of you, be careful not to burn yourselves." He thrusts the sticks into the bonfire flames and hands them back to the boys.

Niki twirls his stick, forming what looks like a hoop of fire, then shouts, "May Baba be healthy and have a long life." His friends yell similar blessings for their friends and family.

Baba smiles, then glances at the dancers. "The *horo* tonight is wilder than usual."

"Since it's the last one until Easter, everyone wants to enjoy themselves," Maria says.

When the small fires burn down, boys jump over the ashes.

Niki shuffles over and plops down next to Baba and his parents. "Do those fires protect us from illness like on *Baba Marta Den*?"

"They do, and they'll also keep fleas out of the house, and make sure we don't have drenching summer rains that ruin the crops," Maria says.

"Oh." Niki's head droops. "Are we going home soon?"

"Yes," Georgi says. "Here comes Rada." He waves to her. "We want to get home before the boys burn the yard with their arrows."

"Oh, Dad!" She says. "No boys are going to shoot arrows in our yard saying how much they love me."

"I don't know. I saw a few looking your way during the *horo*." Georgi wraps his arm around her shoulder. "They better not get too close or be too vulgar. When I shoot the shotgun at midnight, I might announce more than the arrival of Lent."

"I'm not interested in any boys is this village. I have bigger dreams."

"I left a bucket of water on the porch just in case."

Older boys linger by the bonfire, getting their arrows ready. They hand-carved them weeks ago so they'd be dry enough to burn tonight. One boy thrusts his arrow into the flames, then attaches the arrow to the launching pad, points it in the direction of a girl's house, and shouts, "Rada Pavlova! Let the old priest come. I send my white arrow flying to my girl. Let her give me a white cradle in return." He lets the flaming arrow fly.

Rada blushes.

Georgi chuckles. "See, what did I tell you?"

Rada huffs, then hurries home to put out the flames before they burn the yard or worse.

# Kukerovden

*March 14 – Кукеровден – Kukerovden: Mummer's Day.
Кукер – Kuker (singular), kukeri (plural): Mummers, the men who participate in the ritual.
<u>Monday, first day of Lent.</u>
*In some areas, it's celebrated on New Year's Eve; in others on Shrovetide to mark the beginning of Lent.*
*A moveable holiday that depends on when Easter is celebrated.*

*Kukerovden* is a festive, noisy, and somewhat frightful celebration. *Kukeri*, the men who participate in the ritual, dress in furry costumes like wild animals and wear colorful, wooden masks with scary faces, mostly of rams, goats, or bulls. The men parade through the village; they jump and yell, perform skits about plowing and sowing seeds, and pantomime political and other popular figures. As they move in special rhythmic steps, giant bells around their waists clang loudly.

The *kukeri* originally performed their rituals and games for a variety of reasons: scare away spirits released on the winter solstice, harness nature's reviving energy so fields become fertile, and demonstrate their own ability to produce offspring. Today, it's mostly for fun.

Traditionally, only men participated in the celebration. In many villages, the privilege of being a *kuker* was passed from father to son. Each man had to learn to dance first. Only then would the entire group judge if he was worthy to join.[9]

## ~ ORIGINS ~

The *kukeri* celebration is one of the oldest surviving traditions that can be traced to Dionysian rites, symbolizing life, death, and rebirth. Thracian warriors believed if they dressed in animal skins, they could battle against spirits that threatened the Sun's rebirth. By performing rituals, warriors could either scare spirits away or capture their powers. With these powers, men renewed nature's strength, when the earth awakened after a long winter. They believed that only men, who carried the seed of life in their bodies, had the ability to rouse and nurture the female Mother Earth, preparing her for the sowing of seeds.

## ~ RITUALS IN PRACTICE ~

A multitude of bells ring as the parade of masked, furry men nears the Pavlov house.

"Dad!" Niki dashes from the window. "We have to hurry to join the other *kukeri*!"

Georgi buckles a leather belt. Several large cow bells on it dangle over his full-body, sheep-skin costume. "Stand still a moment, and I'll help you finish." He slips a hand-carved mask of a snarling ram over his son's face. Its frightening eyes are painted red, and twisting horns jut from the forehead. "Remember, we can't talk while we're in the parade."

Niki's head bobs all over the place, shaking and nodding at the same time. "Why?"

---

[9] Mishkova, Iglika. "Dreaming of Mummers/Survashkari." https://www.academia.edu/10066480/Dreaming_of_Mummers_Survashkari.

"Not really sure. It's always been taboo to do that." Georgi straightens his belt. "Perhaps it's because with all the noise, no one would hear us anyway."

Niki dances around the room, the light-weight bells on his belt jingling.

"And one more thing," Georgi says. "Don't take your mask off until after the parade."

Niki stops jumping. "Why?"

"I know this answer. Because the masks have power to protect us from harm."

"Protect us from harm?" Niki's eyes brighten, and he runs from the room saying, "Rada!"

A moment later, someone screams. Georgi grabs his own mask and hurries to see what's the matter.

Rada clutches Niki by the sheepskin on his costume's arm, dragging him into the living room. "I woke to *this*," pointing to Niki's mask, "in my face."

Georgi laughs and removes Rada's hand from Niki. "I seem to recall you did the same thing to Baba with my mask when you were his age." He takes his mask and snaps its jaws. "At least the jaws on Niki's mask don't move, so he couldn't bite you the way you bit Baba with mine."

"It was only a little nip," Rada says, blushing. "She was able to cover the red mark it left on her ear with her hair."

"Let's go, young *kuker*." Georgi slips his mask over his head. Calling back to Rada, he says, "Tell your mother and Baba we'll see them after the parade at the games."

The two males join the other *kukeri*. Balkan tags along as the men dance around the village to the tune of bagpipes, flutes, and drums.

## Did you know...?

In the past, kukeri *have scared more than spirits. When the Ottoman Empire ruled Bulgaria, a group of Turkish soldiers once surrounded a rebel leader and his followers. To terrify the soldiers, the rebels donned masks, put bells around their waists, and made torches of hemp soaked in tar. At dusk they crept toward the enemy camp. The soldiers scattered when they saw what they thought were devils who carried long forks and breathed fire.*

Maria wakes soon after the men leave. She and Rada begin the task of thoroughly cleaning the house and dishes.

"I think 'Clean Monday' is my least-favorite part of this holiday," Rada says while scrubbing pots and pans.

"It was mine, too, when I was your age." Maria scours the oven. "But it's Lent. It's not just that we can't eat meat, we have to get rid of any trace of meat and fat from the house."

"I wish Niki had to help instead of running around having fun all day," Rada grumbles.

Maria puts down her sponge, rises, and hugs Rada. "That's not our way. Maybe you can bring new traditions into your family when you have one."

## Message of the Two-Faced Mask

Later that day, the *kukeri* make their way back to the Pavlov house. Music and clanging bells announce their arrival. The women sit on the porch as the men approach.

"When I was young," Baba says, "the *kukeri* visited homes only after it turned dark. We had a saying. 'Don't let the sun catch us on the road.' "

Rada pulls her chair closer. "Why did you say that?"

"The sun was important in ancient rituals." Baba closes her eyes, pausing. "The *kukeri* got up early to chase spirits with loud bells. If they didn't do this, the spirits could steal the sun's power, and then it wouldn't be able to rise. That would be disaster for everyone. Without the sun, crops wouldn't grow, and people would starve."

Baba rocks the chair, eyes still closed, listening to the noisy men.

Rada touches her hand. "Look, Baba. A two-faced mask."

Completely covered with animal skins and a huge mask, the man is unrecognizable. As he dances around, both sides of the colorful mask come into the women's view. The front shows a hooked nose, slanted eyes, and grimace revealing gaping teeth. The back image has a stub nose, is smiling, and has wide, round eyes.

"I wonder if that's Adrian." Maria peers closely. "I'm sure that's Yordan with Niki right next to him, because I *know* that's Balkan barking at them."

"Do you know why that mask has two faces?" Baba asks.

Maria gestures for Rada to respond.

"Tell me, please."

"The ugly face is wickedness; the happy face is goodness." Baba stares at the mask for a while. "They're both sides of human nature. And not only humans. The earth itself. The seasons. The mask exemplifies duality and how both good and evil exist in harmony in our lives."

**Kukeri and the Witch's Magic**

"Will you tell me the legend about the *kukeri* and the witch's magic?" Rada glances at the performers, then back at Baba. "At least then Niki won't have all the fun."

Baba clears her throat. "Once Zliyana, an evil daughter of a northern king fell in love with Dobrodor, a good ruler of our land."

"Were those really their names or only symbolic?" Rada asks. "Zliyana means 'evil maker,' and Dobrodor means 'maker of good.' "

"Perhaps both. Names are important. Sometimes people become like their names," Baba says. "Or perhaps Zliyana only became evil after Dobrodor spurned her. She sent him wonderful gifts, but he returned those tokens of her love."

"Why did he do that?"

"A kind, beautiful woman had captured his heart."

Rada snorts. "And Zliyana wasn't kind or beautiful?"

"She wasn't after that," Baba says. "She lived up to her name and decided to bring evil on Dobrodor and his people. She cast a spell to make all unmarried men die if they tilled the fields. Since it was springtime, some men disregarded the warning. They fell to the ground dead as soon as their ploughs dug into the earth."

"I bet that frightened the rest of them."

"Yes, it did. They begged Dobrodor to do something. They would die of starvation if they couldn't plant their fields."

"What could he do if she was using magic?" Rada asks.

"To prevent any more deaths, Dobrodor told all the unmarried men to disguise themselves. Some donned women's clothing, while others pretended to be animals. They tied bells around their waists and wore masks made from goat skins."

"Not wooden masks like we have today?"

"No, Rada. People made those many years later to make the masks last longer," Baba explains. "The men who were dressed as women harnessed the ones clothed as animals and drove the ploughs through the fields. The witch's magic was fooled, seeing not men, but only women and animals in the field."

"She couldn't have been a powerful witch if her magic was fooled so easily."

## *Did you know...?*

*In some villages, people make new masks each year. In places where* kukeri *don't wear wooden masks, they cover their faces with cloth or blacken them with coal.*

### *Kukeri* Games

Georgi and Adrian come forward and pantomime plowing and sowing a field. The women cheer, their voices becoming hoarse as they try to be heard above the music and bells.

A couple of other men rock back and forth. Baba explains their actions. "They're pretending to be heavy ears of corn weighed down on their stalks."

When another group of men jump into the air, she says, "They're showing us how tall crops are going to grow." A couple others roll on the ground. "Now those two. They're drawing strength from the soil."

"What about Niki and Yordan? What are they doing?" Rada points as the boys dance around, swinging wooden clubs at each other in mock battle, with Balkan running around, trying to get between them.

Baba smiles. "How appropriate. They're fighting against spirits." Baba cranes her neck to look at the activities of others. "Oh my!"

"What's wrong?" Maria leans closer.

Baba cups her hand to her mouth and whispers, "See the ones pretending to conceive and give birth to a baby? We shouldn't let Rada see."

"Baba, I know all about that." Rada peeks and then blushes. "Maybe you could tell me about the *kukeri* masks. What do all the colors, threads, and fabrics attached to them mean?"

The men finish their skits and Maria stands. "While she tells you, I'll get the performers' gifts."

"Let's see." Baba purses her lips. "The colors. Red is the sun's fire." She twists in her seat to look at Rada. "Have I already told you how important the sun was?"

"Yes, Baba. Without it, we'd have no crops and we'd all die."

"Yes. That's true." Baba waves to Niki, who waves back, then continues his sword play. "Black is the earth, and white is water."

"Just like on our clothing." Rada looks at her embroidered dress and apron.

"Exactly." Baba beams and leans back in her chair. "You're good to listen to an old lady's tales."

"How else am I going to let my own grandchildren know unless I learn from you?"

Baba grasps Rada's hand and squeezes. "Now where was I?"

"You told me about the colors," Rada replies. "You were going to tell me why they're important."

"Red, black, and white. Sun, earth, water. These are the elements essential for restoring fertility to the land after winter." She looks up as Maria returns to hand out bread and wine to the *kukeri*. "That's what this celebration is all about. The never-ending cycle of life."

The parade of men continues past to the next house. Following the *kukeri* are carts carrying men dressed in women's clothes and others impersonating celebrities and political figures. They act out satires of political and social issues.

Maria sits again and laughs at their antics. "I love the *smeshnitsi*. They really are funny men."

Next, a bride, groom, and priest pass by on foot, followed by the mother- and father-in-law making angry gestures.

Baba turns to Rada. "That's one ugly bride."

"Shh. That's Simeon."

The boy winks at Rada, and she gives him a shy wave.

Other men walk by, dressed as doctors, policemen, a king, and even a bear and its trainer. Finally the last one passes the house.

"Go ahead and follow them if you want, Rada." Maria rises and holds her hand out to her mother-in-law. "I'll stay here with Baba and go to the village center for the final skit."

"I will, but first I want Baba to finish telling me about all the things the *kukeri* attach to their masks." She gets out of her chair and holds open the door, following the two older women inside.

Baba sits in her rocker, pulls an afghan onto her lap, and waits for Rada to sit on the couch. "The *kukeri* like to add shiny objects onto their masks. Mirrors especially. These scare demons as much as the bells do."

"What about ivy and basil?" Rada asks.

"Ivy. That's something that goes back to our Thracian ancestors. It was sacred to Dionysus. He often wore a crown made from it."

"Why did he choose ivy?"

"You know how long winters can be here," Baba says. "Ivy flourishes year round. But it's more than that. It's a plant associated with forbidden passion. The more you restrict its growth, the more it creeps and spreads everywhere. Like the wild ceremonies honoring the god of wine, once they started, they grew into a frenzy, and only stopped when the Maenads tore the sacrificial animal ... or person ... to pieces."

Rada shivers. "Too bad Niki's not here. He loves that part of the story."

"Now basil," Baba says, her eyes shining as she looks toward Rada. "That's used for love. Today's celebration is also to wish those you love health and happiness."

Rada stands and bends to kiss her grandmother. "I wish you health and happiness."

"Thank you, my dear. Now run along and have a good time with your friends."

## Final Skit

Later in the day after the *kukeri* have paraded to all the houses, Maria and Baba find Rada in the village center where *kukeri* still dance and jump, making a racket. The women bring more gifts of food for the feast after the games. Any leftover money the *kukeri* received as they visited each household will be given to charities.

"Let's sit over there." Maria points to a bench by the circle of rocks enclosing the area where the final skit will take place. "That way Baba doesn't have to stand for long."

Niki spots his mother and runs over. Balkan trots behind him. Niki squeezes himself between Maria and Baba, then drops his club and mask on the ground. "I've had a blast!"

"I can see that." Maria runs her fingers through his sweat-soaked hair. "Stay here now and watch the play with us. Baba can tell you what's happening."

The men, still dressed in their costumes, straggle into the enclosed area. Niki begins his onslaught of questions. "Baba, why do they have the play in a circle? To keep little kids out?"

"No, although I'm sure they thought of that, too." Baba laughs. "The circle of stones symbolizes a cave."

"A cave?" Niki scoffs, his head moving quickly in disbelief. "It doesn't look like a cave."

"That's what symbolize means. It's not the real thing, just pretend." She touches her fingertips together, rounding them at the top. Where the thumbs and index fingers meet, it forms an opening. "See, a circle. A cave."

"Awesome!" Niki does the same. "Why would they have it in a cave anyway?"

"You know that today's celebration is all about making crops grow, right?"

"Yah."

"And you've seen how human and animal babies grow inside their mother."

Niki turns away. "Uh-huh."

"Well, that's what the cave is like for the land. It's Earth's womb."

Niki jumps up and waves. "There's Dad! He said he was going to sow seeds."

Maria and Baba laugh at Niki's choice of words.

Behind Georgi, the lead *kuker* enters the circle. He's covered with animal skins, and a red-painted wooden phallus sways from the middle of his belt.

"Why is his outfit different?" Niki glances at the other *kukeri*, then returns his attention to the first one.

Baba says, "His costume's made of seven different sheep pelts. One covers each limb, and the other three are on his back, front, and head. And—"

"That's it!" Niki says. "He has fur on his head instead of a mask. And a horn sticking out of his forehead." He places a fist on his own head and pretends to butt an invisible enemy.

"In this play, that lets us know he's going to play Dionysus," Baba says.

"Does he get to drink a lot of wine the way Dad did on *Trifonovden*?" Niki covers his mouth and snickers. "He was certainly grumpy the next day. Everyone had to talk softly."

"No. Other interesting things will happen to the *kuker*, though. Sit and watch, and I'll tell you what's going on."

Niki sits on the seat next to her. "Baba, I know some. Let me tell you."

"Okay. Which skit first?"

"The guys with the jangling bells over there," he points, "are scaring the bad spirits. Like Rada."

"Hey, I heard that! Watch it. You don't have your mask on to protect you now."

Niki sticks out his tongue. "The ones closest to us are oxen, pulling a plow around the circle."

"And the man behind them? What's he doing?"

"He's planting seeds." Niki imitates the man by pretending to reach into a bucket and scattering seeds on the ground.

## Did you know...?

*Dionysus invented the plow. At least he was the first to yoke oxen to one. Before that, people dragged the device by hand. This god of wine was also in charge of vegetation, which is why traditions put so much emphasis on soil's fertility.*

"Very good," Baba says. "Look what's happening now."

Several *kukeri* chase after the lead man. They wave their swords in his direction.

"They're trying to kill him." Niki keeps his eyes directed toward the men.

"That's right. They're Titans. Hera, the queen of the gods, ordered them to kill Dionysus because ... she didn't like his mother, Semele."

"That's so mean." Rada shudders.

"Not if he was annoying like you are sometimes." Niki cranes his head around Baba and takes a quick peek at Rada before returning to watch the Titans slash at Dionysus with their wooden swords.

The Titans pretend to tear the god's body apart. They toss it over the plow and tie him down while the oxen continue to pull the plow, tilling the soil. Men dressed as women plant seeds on the god. Finally, the slain man jumps up, his bells ringing.

"The god's alive again," Baba says.

The man holds out his hands, and other *kukeri* remove the animal skins.

Balkan growls and barks, then runs after a cat.

## Did you know...?

*In Thracian times, people identified dogs and wolves as the winter face of the Sun God.*

"Come back!" Niki springs up and rushes after him.

Maria turns to Rada. "Will you make sure the two of them don't get into trouble?"

"Sure, Mom." She rises and heads in the direction Niki went.

Maria slides closer to Baba. "You lost your audience. You can tell me stories if you want."

Baba smiles. "I think you know them well by now. I'm rather tired anyway. We can watch for once."

"I wonder whose fields they'll bury the pelts in," Maria says.

"I hope one goes to Andrei. He had trouble growing crops last year. His family can use the extra luck it'll bring to make the soil fertile."

"Speaking of fertilizing." Maria points to a new skit. "It's a good thing Rada and Niki left."

The previously slain *kuker* chooses one of the men dressed as a woman and mimics "fertilizing" his "bride" with the wooden phallus. The bride grasps her swollen stomach, moans, then pulls a kitten from inside her skirt.

"Talk about having a kitten." Maria laughs.

The *kuker* glances around the audience. He stops when he looks toward Kamelia, then he approaches her. After removing the wooden phallus from his belt, he touches her on the shoulder with it and hands it to her husband.

"It looks like Kamelia and Mihael may finally have children." Baba smiles. "We need more babies here. So many young people keep moving away."

Maria stands. "I wonder where my babies went. I'll go look for them. Georgi should be here soon to keep you company."

"That looks like Niki by the fire with the older boys." Baba points and Maria goes to retrieve her son.

One boy backs away from the fire, then runs forward and leaps over it, yelling, "Mother Earth, expel sinister forces from the land."

They thump each other on the backs while glancing toward a group of young girls. "See how strong the fire's made us!"

Georgi, still in his costume, dances over to his mother. He removes his mask. "What a day. Did you enjoy yourself?"

"Yes, son," Baba says. "Your children let me entertain them with stories."

Niki returns, with Maria steps behind him. "Do you have more stories to tell me today, Baba?"

"Maybe another day. Let's watch everyone dance."

Maria joins hands with Georgi. "We'll eat after the *horo*." They leave and form a circle with the other dancers. Everyone clasps hands. They twirl around the enclosure, shouting and moving their feet with quick kicking motions.

Rada returns and sits next to Baba and Niki. "I'll dance later. I'll stay here if you want to go back with your friends, Niki."

Niki runs off and Baba sighs. "We used to have so many other traditions today."

"Don't be sad, Baba. We can make new traditions together." Rada leans into her and wraps her arm around her grandmother's waist.

# Todorovden

**\*March 19 – Тодоровден – Todorovden: St. Todor's Day, Horse Easter.**
**Тодорова събота – Todorova sŭbota: St. Todorova Saturday.**
<u>First Saturday of Lent.</u>
*St. Todor, or Theodore of Amasea. Patron of soldiers, the recovery of lost articles, and protection against storms. Martyred 306 A.D. He was imprisoned after he burned a pagan temple to the ground. He was beaten, burned, and had his eyes removed before he was finally crucified and killed by the sword to speed his death.*
*\*A moveable holiday that depends on when Easter is celebrated.*

**St. Todor**

During most of Lent, dancing is forbidden, but the ban on festivities is lifted for **Todorovden**, near the beginning of the season, and *Lazarovden*, at the end. Like many holidays, *Todorovden* honors a saint, but also has other rituals mixed into the day's celebrations. St. Todor shares his day with horses, which are an integral part of farm work in many Bulgarian villages. This gives the day its other name: Horse Easter.

People decorate horses with tassels and beads, then enter them into a horserace, *kushia*. To demonstrate their horses' strength, owners complete them in contests where horses pull trees, the winner being the one that pulls it the farthest.

## ~ ORIGINS ~

This holiday is on the brink of winter and spring, a time when people looked for explanations about why the seasons changed. One legend rationalized it by telling how St. Todor put on nine fur coats to keep warm against the winter wind, mounted his horse, and set off to find God, all to beg him for summer's arrival.

But, it's not so much his riding the horse that gives this holiday its more popular name. That comes from the time of the Thracians. Mention of their horses goes back to the *Illiad* where Homer writes about Thracian King Rhesus. "He has the tallest, finest horses I ever saw, whiter than snow and fast as the wind."

Homer also called Thracians "a race of horsemen." Not only did they breed horses for racing, the nation also used them in warfare, both when they traveled as mercenaries, as well as when they engaged in internal fighting.

## ~ RITUALS IN PRACTICE ~

Today, Rada takes over the task of making bread, always an important part of every Bulgarian celebration. She shapes the rolls like hooves, twisting the dough around itself so it looks more like toes.

Baba laughs. "Clever."

Before long, the smell of baking bread drifts through the house, waking Niki. Rubbing his eyes, he shuffles into the kitchen. "Can I have one?"

"Sure, but only one for now."

He breaks it open and takes a bite. Steam pouring out forms tiny droplets on his face. "Mmm. I love bread."

"If you get dressed, you can come with me to church. You'll enjoy running around pretending to be a horse while I give them out."

Niki shakes his head in agreement, and stuffs the rest of the roll into his mouth. "Yeth, pleathe."

## Did you know...?

*When a Bulgarian nods his head up and down it means "no," and shaking his head from side to side means "yes."*

"Breakfast first, Niki," Maria says. "Then you can help Rada."

Rada finishes the rolls while Niki eats. She decorates them with walnuts, garlic, and salt, then puts them into a basket, covering it with a cloth. She sets one plain roll aside to mix with the horse feed to bring the animal luck in the race. "Ready?"

"Yes." He hurries to put on a jacket.

On their way to the church, they meet girls, and young women married for less than a year heading in that direction. Rada and Niki rush so they won't be the last.

"While I run around handing out the rolls, you can prance like a horse. Okay?" Rada says.

Niki whinnies and jumps, scraping his feet against the ground.

"Sometimes a little brother comes in handy." Rada smiles as she hands him another roll. "I'd feel rather foolish doing that."

She scurries from one person to the next, saying, "May your horses be healthy this year."

## Did you know...?

*After the horse race on* Todorovden, *girls collect the first rain that pools in the hoof prints. They use this or straw from the horse's manger when they wash their hair. Both are guaranteed to make their hair grow as long and thick as a horse's mane.*

Niki trails, pretending to be a lively horse. When all her rolls are gone, Rada sits at a table to catch her breath. Nearby, three recently married women begin the ceremony to end the "reverential silence" toward their mothers-in-law. Each of the women wraps a white scarf around her forehead, stands in front of her mother-in-law, and bow three times.

"Rada?" Niki asks. "Why are they bowing? This isn't *Sirni Zagovezni.*"

"It's a sign of respect, the same as on *Sirni Zagovezni,*" Rada says. "You would have laughed at what they did last night."

"What?" Niki's eyes grow big.

"Each woman who got married last year dresses in her wedding outfit, and goes to church with her mother-in-law."

Niki snorts. "That's not interesting. We always go to church."

"Let me finish." Rada taps him on the shoulder. "The mother-in-law carries boiled corn inside to get it blessed. The brides have to wait outside."

"We get things blessed all the time, too," Niki says.

"You'll like this next part. The mother-in-law kicks the bride when she comes out."

"What? Why?" His mouth drops open.

"It's just a little kick, like a horse, since this is Horse Easter," Rada explains. "Then they spread the corn over their gardens so they'll have a good harvest."

"Do you think Baba kicked Mom?"

"I'm sure she did."

Niki puts his hand over his mouth and snickers. "She kicked Mom."

"Shh. We're missing the ceremony," the woman next to Rada and Niki scolds.

Each bride takes the hand of her mother-in-law and greets her. After months of silence, as a sign of respect, each woman can now speak to her husband's mother.

"You excited about the *kushia* yet?" Rada asks.

"Yes." He bobs up and down on the seat. "I'm going to help Dad make the wreath to put on our horse. I'm sure it'll win the race. It's so strong." He flexes his muscles. "Just like me."

Rada raises her eyebrows. "Someday, I'm sure." She stands and holds her hand out to him. "Let's go back and get ready. I'll make you some lentils and mushroom soup for lunch."

"When do I get to race a horse?" Niki pouts.

"I think you have to be a few years older first." She heads toward home. "Did Dad say who was riding our horse this year?"

"Peter Kristof." Niki puts the last of his roll into his mouth and chews. "Why doesn't Dad ride?"

"He's married, silly. Only single men race." Rada bites her lip as she walks down the road. "I wonder why Peter never married. He's *Mom's* age after all."

## The *Kushia*

With the noon meal over, the Pavlov family gathers in the meadow. Georgi lifts Niki so he can place the floral wreath around their horse's neck. Rada ties ribbons and beads along the reins, pats the horse's neck, and joins the other young people. They form a circle around all the horses and riders. When the music begins, they perform a *horo*, singing songs and wishing the riders luck. Then they break the circle, and the race begins.

The riders race across the meadow to the sound of bagpipes and drums. Peter pulls out in front.

Georgi groans. "Not so soon."

In a short time, other horses catch up, and two pass Peter right before the finish line.

"Third's not so bad." Maria kisses Georgi's cheek. "Damyan can use the new shirt the winner gets. He doesn't have a wife yet to make him one."

A young woman ties a multi-colored scarf around the winning horse's neck, then hands new reins and an embroidered shirt to Damyan. He watches her as she turns to leave.

Maria nudges Georgi. "Maybe Damyan won't be able to participate next year. You better get ready for the log pulling. Maybe you'll win that. Your horse is as strong as a Thracian-bred one."

Georgi rises and walks toward Peter. Before Peter can speak, Georgi says, "You did your best. Want to help me rub the stallion down?"

"Yes."

The two men groom the horse, then hook it to a cart. They pull up to the starting line. To the back of the cart, they attach the trunk of a felled tree. Georgi waits for the signal to begin. The skirl of the *gaida* fills the air, and the men urge the horses ahead. The race is close, but once again Damyan's horse wins by pulling the trunk the farthest.

Damyan unhitches the cart, mounts his horse, and trots past. The villagers head to their homes to await his visit as the winner of the race. They'll pour blessings on him and offer his horse water, then wait for the *horo* to end the day's festivities.

At the dance that evening, Damyan begins the horo. Then the new brides and their mothers-in-law join hands and dance, while onlookers sing songs summoning spring.

## Magical Horses

*Ancient Thracians were well known for their horses. They venerated the animals, considering them mystical creatures that carried men back and forth from the underworld, spoke to give advice, and predicted their master's future. Thracians believed the animals were immune to spirits and sickness, and could safely transport people through forests and by rivers and lakes where spirits dwelt at night.*

*Some customs dealing with horses were:*

- *When a ruler died, his horse was buried with him.*
- *Women embroidered images of horses onto clothing to protect family during travels.*
- *Heroes took oaths on their weapons and their horses.*
- *The Proto Bulgarians used horses in battles. They took inventory of ammunition, troops, and horses.*

# Blagovets

**March 25 – Благовец – Blagovets: Annunciation, means "Good News." Also called "Half Easter."**
**Самодива – Samodiva (singular), Samodivi (plural): Woodland nymphs from Bulgarian lore whose name means "Wild alone." Also called Vili or Vily, Samovili, and Veelas.**
*This is the official feast of the Annunciation, the day the angel Gabriel told Mary she would give birth to the Savior. In folklore, the good news extends beyond the Eastern Orthodox Church to rituals of spring, dating back to Thracian times.*

Spring is a magical time as the earth blooms with life again. The season's rituals are filled with enchantment, mystery, and taboos. **Blagovets** is the Bulgarian holiday closest to the vernal equinox, the official arrival of spring. A popular saying is that not even mammals, birds, or insects work on this day while people wait for nature to give birth to spring.

The cuckoo plays an important role in beliefs and rituals since its song announces spring's arrival. On a darker note, according to Bulgarian folklore, hearing the cuckoo sing is a warning that wild, beautiful *Samodivi*, who have enchanted Bulgarians for centuries, have also returned. Not only *Samodivi*, but mermaids, dragons, and other mystical creatures also return from their secret winter village in Zmeykovo, or Dragon Village, to the human world, where they live until late fall. Other sources say *Samodivi* have their own winter home called Kushkundalevo or Omayniche, a place only magpies know how to find.

Bulgarians pay special homage to *Samodivi*. These female nymphs of the woodlands and waterways like to play tricks on people and even carry them away as prisoners, although sometimes a *Samodiva* befriends a human depending on her mood. To avoid having these wild, capricious ladies harm or kidnap their daughters, mothers don't let them near bodies of water in the morning because that's where *Samodivi* gather.

## Did you know...?

*The name* Samodiva *translates to "wild alone." (*Samo *means "alone," and* diva *is "wild.")* Diva *also comes from "divine," and "alone" signifies the nymphs prefer to avoid interaction with people.*

It's not only these lovely nymphs people worry about. Spring is also the time snakes slither out of their lairs to warm themselves in the sun. These creatures play a double role in celebrations. Families consider the ones living under their home's threshold guardians and protectors, while all other snakes are a menace. On *Blagovets*, women and children chase the creatures with loud noises. Children also "singe" their own heels in a purifying fire to avoid being bitten by snakes—a true Achilles' heel.

## ~ ORIGINS ~

Snakes and birds fill Bulgarian folklore. Both creatures represent the continuation of life and eternity. The snake, pictured with its tail in its mouth, becomes a circle, the symbol of no beginning or ending. In addition, the outer appearance of snakes and birds change, with birds molting and snakes shedding their skin. This portrays life, death, and rebirth.

People also believed snakes and birds traveled between the realms of the World Tree: birds flew between heaven and earth, and snakes crawled from the underworld to the earth. This mystical quality associated them with the gods themselves in many ancient religions. By living in the roots of the World Tree, or the underworld, snakes depicted the dark side of life. Their image of being sly, deceitful creatures dates back to antiquity. The story of Satan disguising himself as a serpent to tempt Eve in the garden of Eden is well known in much of the world.

## *Did you know...?*

*Snakes were the symbol of the king in the Thracian religion.*

Lesser recognized is the snake's more benevolent side. Since roots are also part of the earth itself, peopled revered snakes for their connection to the soil, which provides a fruitful harvest. Legends portray snakes as wise, with vast knowledge of healing plants and an understanding of the language of animals. People believed that only on *Blagovets* could snakes teach these mysteries to humans.

Cuckoos, another herald that winter is departing and spring has arrived, represent love and maidenhood, with many religions associating the bird to Mother Goddess worship. In Greek mythology, the cuckoo is Hera's bird. Before Hera became queen of the gods, Zeus, disguised as a forlorn cuckoo, came to her. She took pity on the creature and held it to her chest. The god transformed to his normal self and seduced her. Dishonored, she was shamed into marrying him.

The origins of *Samodivi* vary, and at times *Samodivi* and *Samovili* are interchanged. However, each type of nymph has a key difference. *Samovili* were born spirits of the forests. They dislike humans and seek to harm them.

On the other hand, one source says *Samodivi* were once human women, who neither heaven nor hell wanted after their death. Usually, this was because they died tragically before they were married or baptized. Other legends say women joined the sisterhood of *Samodivi* after other *Samodivi* kidnapped them.

Some legends say *Samodivi* were born from a *lamia*, female dragon. Other stories claim they were daughters of the Thracian goddess Bendis, often associated with Artemis, a Greek goddess of the hunt, who protected nature. As such, *Samodivi* have a special connection with nature and spring. They have power to heal using herbs, and so their role is to protect forests and their inhabitants. They are a symbol of the coming spring, the awakening of nature.

Like so many Bulgarian traditions originating from the Thracians, a cosmic element surrounds *Samodivi*. Their "free, untamed spirit" is a necessary element that helps maintain the universe's balance.[10]

## ~ RITUALS IN PRACTICE ~

On the eve of *Blagovets*, the Pavlov house is once again a bustle of activity. Rada and Maria dash from room to room cleaning and collecting stray papers and other unwanted items. They put them into a willow basket. Niki watches the commotion from the couch.

"Baba?" He swivels to face his grandmother, who's in her favorite rocker. "Why are they picking up papers? Are we going to jump over another fire?"

"Yes, you're observant."

"We did that a few weeks ago. Is it *Baba Marta Den* again?"

"No, tomorrow's *Blagovets*," Baba says. "Tossing trash into the fire is a way to burn illness from the coming year."

Georgi lifts the basket Rada and Maria filled. "And we have a special ceremony for you to do." He chuckles as he puts the trash on the porch.

"What?" Niki asks his grandmother, but looks to where his father exited. "Is it fun?"

"You'll see tomorrow after breakfast." Baba smiles. "Your father will help you with it."

Niki peers out the window. The moment his father returns, he asks, "Dad, what kind of ceremony?"

**Treasure Hunting**

"Something to protect you from snake bites." Georgi pats Niki on the head. "Right now, how about you come with me to look for buried treasure."

"Wow! Really?" He rushes to the door. "Let's go."

"Put your jacket on. It's chilly out." Maria holds the garment for Niki to slip his arms into. She turns to Georgi. "Don't keep him out too late. I don't want you out in the woods when the *Samodivi* return."

"Dad, let's stay out to see them!" Niki tugs on his father's sleeve. "Please! I've never seen one."

Georgi looks from Maria's stern, frightened expression to Niki's eager one, and shrugs his shoulders. "I'll take good care of him. We'll be back soon. It's only starting to get dark now. We have plenty of time. The *Samodivi* won't arrive until tomorrow."

"At least stay away from their *cheshma* by the spring. I've heard stories of people seeing them by that fountain."

"All right. I won't go near it. I'll take the old path. Legends say the Turks from the Ottoman Empire used that one to transport gold." He kisses Maria. "It goes to the meadow where the wild horses graze. No water nearby at all. There's an old walnut tree there. I'm sure someone buried treasure near it."

"I want to find gold." Niki hops around his parents. "Let's go before anyone else gets there first."

Maria smiles at her son's eagerness. "My grandmother told me that story, too. Bulgarian rebels attacked the Turks and stole the gold. She said it was in her village, though. Under an old tree near a *cheshma* called *Bivola*. It was named that because a black bull guarded the gold at night."

"I'm sure the tree in the meadow here is as old as the one in your grandmother's village." Georgi leans closer and whispers, "At least it will get Niki out of your way for a bit."

"Mom! Dad! I want to hurry to find the gold!" Niki rattles the door handle.

Maria laughs. "You better go before you have to fix the door." She lays her hand on Georgi's shoulder. Her voice trembles. "Please be careful. Both of you."

---

[10] Milkova, Stiliana, "Walled-in Wives, Dragon's Brides, and Wild Fairies: Women in the Bulgarian Folk Tradition," in *Forum Folkloristika*, Eastern European Folklife Center, Inaugural Edition, Issue 1, Spring 2012, https://www.eefc.org/folkloristika_1-1.shtml.

"We will." Georgi picks up his *baklitsa* from the counter. "If we run into a *Samodiva*, I'll pour wine onto the ground. It'll break any spell she can cast on us."

Maria removes a jar of honey from the cupboard and hands it to him. "Leave this at the tree, too. That way, if it's her meadow, she won't enchant you or make you and Niki ill."

He takes the jar. "I will."

## Did you know...?

*Not everyone can see* Samodivi. *A nymph's child can, even if the father was a mortal man. Also people with blue eyes can connect with creatures in the other realms. If you don't fall into either of those categories, you still have a chance to catch a glimpse of a* Samodiva *as she flits from one tree to the other in the forest. Were you born on one of these special days: the Saturday before Easter, All Soul's Day, or at midnight when Christmas Eve becomes Christmas morning? Then you, too, could see a* Samodiva.

A full moon shines onto the dewy grass, making it sparkle as Georgi and Niki step into the meadow. A lantern sways in Georgi's hand. Wild horses nearby continue to graze peacefully.

"Is that the tree?" Niki points to a huge walnut, its budding branches swaying in the breeze.

"That's the one."

Niki scours the ground around the tree, kicking at rocks and other loose objects. "How do we know where the gold is?"

"The coins give off a glow, so look for flashes of blue flames."

Niki peers at the ground while he walks around the tree. "I don't see any."

"Walk away a little. You might be too close."

While Niki backs away a few feet, Georgi drops a coin and a piece of broken pottery onto the ground. With his heel, he pushes the coin under the soil. "What's this?" He bends to pick up the shard.

"Did you find treasure?" Niki runs back.

"Not yet, but legends say it was hidden in clay pottery." He holds up the piece for Niki to inspect. "Why don't you dig in this area for the treasure." He hands Niki a trowel.

Niki scoops up dirt and runs his fingers through it. Not finding any gold, he tosses it aside and pokes the ground again. Finally, he yells to his father, who's digging in a different spot with a shovel. "Dad! Look! I found a lev."

Georgi smiles and takes the coin Niki holds

out. "You've done better than I have." He examines the coin. "It's not the lost gold, but silver will do. If it had been gold, you'd have to throw your shirt over the spot where you found it so you could claim the treasure."

"Why?" Niki takes back the coin.

"The ghosts of the people who buried the gold protect it. Putting something you own over it makes it yours. But if you take the gold, you have to make them an offering of a *kurban*."

"I'd have to give them part of a cooked lamb?" Niki purses his mouth.

"Yes, and you'd have to say, 'A fat lot of use that money will bring.' "

Niki snickers, then continues to dig for more coins. He finds a couple more in places his father suggests he digs. They finally return home, and Georgi puts away the tools.

Beaming, Niki drops the coins on the kitchen table next to Baba. "Look what I found. Treasure!"

"That's wonderful. Hold onto those. You'll need a full stomach and money in your pocket tomorrow before you go outside."

"Why?" Niki asks as he scoops up the coins.

"In case you hear the cuckoo sing," Baba replies. "Then you won't go hungry all year, and you'll have money to spend."

### *Samodivi* – Witches or Goddesses?

"Where's Mom?" Niki slips off his jacket and drapes it over a chair. "I want to tell her I saw a *Samodiva* on the way home."

Maria pops her head into the room. Her face pales. "Y-you d-didn't, c-couldn't. It's too early."

"I did, really." He skips over to her. "I didn't see her close. Only a white flash in the woods."

Maria shivers, grasps Niki's hand tight, and draws it close to her chest.

"Mom." Niki tugs at his hand. "Let go, please."

Maria loosens her grip and turns his hand around. "Go wash. You have dirt caked under your nails."

Georgi wraps his hand around her waist. "It was only a rabbit. The boy has a vivid imagination."

Maria sighs. "I'm going to lie down for a little while."

When Niki returns to the room, everyone's quiet. He sits next to Rada on the couch. "What's wrong with Mom?"

Rada sighs and sets aside a long shirt she's embroidering for the *Lazarovden* ceremony the next month. She stares at Niki.

"What?" He looks at his hands. "I washed them."

Rada laughs. "Not that. It's ... Mom's afraid of *Samodivi*. We all are, actually."

"Why?" Niki asks. "Baba's told me stories about how they protect plants and animals in the forest. They like to ride on female deer, and they have whips made out of snakes." He swings his hands around wildly as if brandishing his own snake whip.

## *Did you know...?*

*The deer or horses* Samodivi *ride have supernatural powers. If a human rides this special creature, he'll obtain great wealth.*

"Yes, that's true. I'm not sure about the snake whips, though." Rada pauses. "A lot of stories talk about good things they do. They heal with herbs. They sometimes even share this knowledge with women who've done them favors."

Baba adds, "*Samodivi* make these women *posestrimi*, sworn sisters. They perform a secret ceremony to initiate the women. It's always done beneath a full moon at midnight on a Sunday."

Niki stops swinging his arms. "And when *Samodivi* aren't riding on deer, they travel by whirlwind." He jumps from the couch and spins around in circles. Balkan runs around with him, until Niki drops to the floor. Balkan lies beside him, resting his nose against Niki's face.

"Sometimes those whirlwinds cause storms at sea, Niki," Baba says. "And men die. Good men. Men with families who need their love and support."

Niki sits up. "Nature causes the wind, not *Samodivi*. I learned about that in school."

"Maybe." Baba covers her legs with her afghan. "Let me tell you a story I heard from my mother. A farmer was out in his field plowing when the winds gusted. Soon they twirled into a whirlwind. It lasted for only about ten seconds, but in that time, a woman's laughter came out of the wind. The farmer was so scared, he ran away. He didn't wait to see what sort of creature came out of the whirlwind when it stopped. He was afraid it was a *Samodiva* who would kidnap him."

Niki slides along the floor, closer to Baba. "Is that what scared Mom? She thought a *Samodiva* would kidnap us?"

"Yes," Baba whispers.

Rada pats the couch seat next to her. "Niki, I want to tell you something that happened several years ago when you were a baby."

Niki sits next to his sister. "What happened?"

"You know Nona, don't you? She's a couple years older than I am."

"Yah, the girl who always wears black and doesn't talk."

"Right," Rada says. "A bunch of us were playing at the beach once and Nona disappeared. No one could find her for weeks. We thought she drowned. But one day she reappeared at the old church. She was dressed in a white gown, with flowers in her hair. She never spoke again after that. We think ... the *Samodivi* had her."

"Is that why she acts so crazy all the time?" Niki looks from his sister to his grandmother. "What did the *Samodivi* do to her?"

"We don't know." Rada twists her apron. "But the point is, you have to be careful. Tomorrow, they return from their secret winter village in Zmeykovo, which is at the end of the world. They won't go back there until the winter solstice."

"You're safe during the day, but at night *Samodivi* come out of their caves. They sing and dance the *horo* in the woods around places where there's water," Baba adds. "If anyone interrupts them, they make the person dance all

night until the person falls down and dies from exhaustion. If he's fortunate, he only becomes ill."

"You remember Mom told Dad to take honey with him when you went out today," Rada says.

"Yah," Niki replies. "*Samodivi* like honey. So do I."

"If they cast a spell that makes you ill, you can encourage them to remove it if you give them gifts," Rada adds. "That's why Mom gave Dad the honey. *Samodivi* also like sweet rolls. I've even heard of people leaving them a horseshoe or basil tied with a red string."

"Baba, Rada, I'm not afraid of them." Niki lifts his head high. "Dad and I'll protect everyone."

"I'm sure you will." Baba smiles. "*Samodivi* aren't always bad. I'll tell you a story about a good one."

"Yes, please," Rada and Niki say together.

Baba takes a deep breath. "Deep in the forests of the Rhodope Mountains in the time when Orpheus and Eurydice lived a happy life in their village, a *Vila-Samodiva* led her sisters in a *horo* dance. Moonlight sparkled on magic flowers that bloomed where their delicate feet touched the ground. Their ethereal white robes made from moonbeams glided in the breeze as the lovely nymphs twirled. Their curly blonde hair streamed over their shoulders like golden waterfalls. A shepherd played his *kaval*, the notes drifting far into the forest. He was not there by choice. One of the *Samodivi* had heard him playing an enchanting tune earlier. Entranced by it, she captured him as he led his sheep home. The only thing *Samodivi* love more than dancing, is dancing with music."

"I like to dance, too." Niki springs up from the couch and bounces around the room.

"Niki, please sit and listen to Baba," Rada scolds.

"Sorry, Baba."

Baba waits until he sits quietly. "As the *Samodivi* danced, a gallant young man came into the clearing. The nymphs lured him toward them with their enchanting songs, enticing him to dance with them. Captivated by their beauty, he was unable to resist. They danced with him until the light of dawn broke over the horizon. As the man fell exhausted to the ground, all the nymphs except the *Vila-Samodiva* fled to the safety of their cave because they feared the light of day. The one who remained looked into his eyes and fell in love with him."

Niki covers his eyes with his hand. "Ugh. A love story."

Rada elbows him, and he becomes silent.

Baba smiles and continues the story. "She carried him into the depths of the forest, where she nursed him back to health. Her sisters warned her to forget about him, to let him die of a broken heart. It was well known that any man who looked into the piercing blue eyes of a *Samodiva* immediately fell in love with her."

Rada glances at Niki to make sure he doesn't interrupt again. He sits holding his stomach, pretending to be ill.

"The *Vila-Samodiva*, however, returned with the man to his home and married him," Baba continues. "She had his children, but she wasn't happy. She missed her sisters and the wild, free life of the forest. Unlike some of her sisters who were forced to live with men who had seized the *Samodivi*'s robes while the nymphs bathed, the *Vila-Samodiva* was free to leave at any time. While her captured sisters had to find their robes before they could flee, the *Vila-Samodiva* had hers hidden. She chose to remain until her children were grown. All of them became mighty heroes because they had the power of the *Samodiva* in their blood. Her husband grew old while she remained forever young and immortal. The *Vila-Samodiva* left him to mourn for her until he died. She shape-shifted into a falcon and flew back to her sisters' cave, vowing to never live a human life again."

## Did you know...?

*A* Samodiva's *power is contained in her white robe, which is called a shadow, or in her belt, which can be golden, green, or rainbow-colored.*

"I want to turn into a bird," Niki says. "That's the best part of the story. It would be fun to fly."

"They can also turn into snakes, swans, wolves, and horses," Rada adds. "Sometimes when they look like women, they have wings."

"Neat! Sort of like an angel." Niki flaps his arms up and down.

"Except not usually as kind as an angel," Baba says. "Other stories tell about *Samodivi* blinding people who have trespassed on their special meadows while they're dancing. I read in the paper about a village where five men mysteriously disappeared while they were in the forest. Only two of them returned, but they couldn't recall anything that happened. They woke up in the forest in the same place they last remembered, but it was two weeks later. Soon after that, one of them started losing his vision."

"Why would they go blind?" Rada asks. "*Samodivi* are beautiful. Not ugly like Medusa with her snake hair that turns people to stone when they look at her."

"*Samodivi* like to play tricks on people who interrupt them. Blindness. Insanity. Death even. It all depends on their mood at the time," Baba says.

## Did you know...?

Samodivi *almost completely disappeared from remote villages when houses installed electricity. Now, instead, other creatures come down on lightning bolts. These energy forces run around even after the storm has passed. Perhaps these sightings began because of the belief in Vila, the Slavic goddess of Energy.*

Maria returns to the room. "We honor them for protecting nature, but they're not like us. It's best to avoid them." She turns to Niki. "Enough stories for tonight. Tomorrow we'll all be up early for *Blagovets*. Baba can tell you more stories then."

Niki yawns and rises from the couch. "Dad said I get to be part of a special ceremony. Will you tell me what it is?"

"Tomorrow will come soon enough," Maria says. "You'll find out then."

## Rites of Spring

The next morning, while the family eats a hearty breakfast, Baba searches the cupboards for pots and pans. She sets several on the counter, then looks at Niki. "Do you want to help us chase snakes and lizards out of the yard?"

"Oh, yes!" He grabs a pan, dashes to his room to get his wooden club, and bangs on the metal.

"Niki!" Rada takes hold of his hands. "Not inside, please."

"When can we go outside?" He sets the pan and club on the counter.

"After we finish eating," Rada replies, then returns to her spot at the table. "Sit back and eat some more. Remember, before you go outside today you have to have a full stomach and—"

"Money in my pocket!" Niki leaves, returning a moment later clutching the coins he found the night before. He shoves them into his pants pocket. "Now I won't be hungry, and I'll have plenty of money to spend this year, but I have to hear the cuckoo sing. Right?"

"I'm glad you listen to some things people tell you," Rada says.

Niki slides into a chair next to her. While he eats, he drums his fingers on the table and bounces his feet against the wooden floor. He takes a sweet bun shaped like a slithering snake from the basket and wiggles it in Rada's face.

"Stop that!" She swats at his hand. "They're to eat, not play with."

"Why did you make them like this if you don't like snakes?" He continues to move the snake through the air.

Maria grasps his hands and sets the bun on his plate. "Because eating a bread replica will protect us from the real snakes."

"Is everyone almost done?" Niki bites the head off the snake, then scrapes his chair across the floor as he gets up. "I want to chase the real snakes."

"Yes, we'll go out now," Baba says. She picks up a pan, then gets a poker from the fireplace.

Maria takes fire tongs and gets a pan, and Rada selects a spoon and one of the remaining pots.

Niki grabs his pot, and retrieves his wooden club from the counter. "Why are you using the fireplace tools?"

"Since they're symbols of the home and family, we can use them to chase snakes and lizards away from our home," Baba says.

Niki bangs on his pot, then stops when Rada takes a step toward him. "Let's go out and chase them."

On the porch, Georgi picks up the basket of papers and other junk. "I'll get the fire started while you get rid of snakes."

The others form a line behind Baba. In parade-like fashion, they walk around the house and shed three times, banging on pans while shouting, "Go away, snakes and lizards. *Blagovets* is here."

Near the shed, Niki yells, "I see one." He chases the snake and whacks it on the head with his club until it stops moving. "I think I killed it. I hope it wasn't the guardian snake."

Baba and Rada come closer, and Maria leaves to join Georgi by the fire.

Baba inspects the snake. "No, it's not our home's protector. He lives under the threshold by the front door."

"Good," Niki says. "I don't want our family to have bad luck."

"Snakes killed today are powerful," Baba says. "If I plant basil seeds in its head, the plant that grows can cure any disease."

"That's awesome." Niki lifts the dead snake and drops it into Baba's pan.

"That thing's nasty." Rada looks at the motionless creature. "But if it had bit you, its poison loses its power today. And besides, all wounds heal quickly today."

"Really?" Niki twists his neck to look at his sister.

"Yes. When I was little, I had my ears pierced on *Blagovets* so they'd heal quicker than normal."

"And we gave you gold studs to protect you from any harm." Baba pokes the snake with a stick. "Did you know the sun is happy when snakes are killed today?"

"Why?" Niki asks. "Was the snake mean to it?"

"Yes. Once a snake was angry that the sun scorched the earth, making it too hot for him to come out of his den. He tried to drink from the sun's eyes to make it less hot."

"What happened?"

"The sun's rays burned the snake. So now the sun is happy every time a snake dies."

Niki picks up the snake's head and tosses it around. "I'm going to drink from the sun's eyes."

Baba laughs. "You can also cast love spells from the basil flowers that grow in a snake's head."

"Yuck." Niki drops the snake back into the pan. "You can use those on Rada, not me."

"No thanks," Rada says. "I want adventures before I get married."

"It can help with headaches, too. Niki, you can help me dig a hole to plant it later today." Baba walks toward Maria and Georgi. "Let's see if the fire's ready for the ceremony now."

"The special one you've been telling me about?" Niki walks next to her.

"Yes, that one."

"Do I get to jump over it again?" Niki stops next to his father.

"Yes," Georgi replies, "but you need to singe your heel to protect yourself from snake bites."

Niki steps away. "You want me to burn myself?"

Georgi motions for Niki to return. "No. Just let the smoke touch your foot. It'll make your heel tougher so a snake can't penetrate the skin with its fangs. You don't actually have to step into the flames or coals the way fire dancers do. I can hold you over it like I did when you were younger."

Niki makes a fist and taps it against his chin. He looks at the fire. "I'll try it myself. I'm not scared." He concentrates on the fire, then leaps over it, keeping his feet close to the flames.

"Good job!" Georgi pats Niki on the back.

"Now everyone else has to do it." Niki looks at Rada.

"The women have other ways to prevent snake bites today. They won't touch anything sharp," Georgi says. "Want to help me start another fire under the apple tree?"

"Do I have to jump over that one, too?"

"No," Georgi replies. "This one will make sure we don't get caterpillars on it."

"We haven't seen a stork yet this year," Maria says, "so we can tie our *martenitsi* onto the tree now. It'll bring us health and good luck for the year. The magic in the charm goes into the tree, so we'll have lots of apples this autumn."

"Yum. I love apples." Niki removes his charm and ties it onto a branch.

"What's even better," Maria adds, "is you can make a wish. It's certain to come true if you make it while you tie your *martenitsa* onto the tree."

Rada removes hers next, then steps back. "It's pretty seeing the charms in the tree. They twirl in the wind like dancing girls."

The others attach their *martenitsi* to branches then return inside.

Maria picks up fresh bread made with honey that Rada baked earlier that morning. "Your father and I are going to go visit Sultana to bring her this."

Niki shivers. "She's a witch."

"No, she's not." Maria sets the bread down and puts her hands on her hips. "She's only a lonely old woman, who's a friend. She's a *znahar* and heals with herbs the way Baba does. You don't think Baba's a witch, do you?"

"No." Niki hangs his head. "I'm sorry."

Maria puts a jacket on and picks up the bread for Sultana and another loaf. "We're going to the vineyard first to bless the soil so we have a good grape harvest this year."

When they leave, Niki sits by Baba on the couch. "How are Mom and Dad going to bless the field?"

"When they get there, your mother will light a small fire near the plow," Baba says. "Fire protects the plow, the same way it protected you when you jumped over it."

"So snakes won't bite the plow?" Niki snickers.

"No," Baba laughs. "That would be funny, wouldn't it? It makes the plow strong so your father can till the soil."

"What does Dad do?"

"He plows a furrow, then he and your mom break a loaf of bread and drop the pieces in. They pour wine over that, cover it, and light a candle on the spot."

Rada sits on the other side of Baba. "That sounds like a romantic picnic. No wonder they didn't invite us to go along."

"Romance," Niki scoffs. "Baba's going to make you drink a love potion from basil flowers that grow out of a snake head."

"She's more likely to plant the seeds in your head, you little snake," Rada responds.

## The Cuckoo's Song

Baba places a hand on Rada and one on Niki. "This is a day you should be careful what you say to each other, and try to get along. Would you like me to tell you a story about what happened to two siblings who fought with each other?"

"Yes," they both say and then become quiet.

"Today is the day you can hear the cuckoo's song," Baba begins. "With her music comes the message that there'll be no more snow or cold winter winds."

"I'm glad," Rada says. "I'm tired of the cold."

"Did you know the bird was once a young girl?" Baba continues.

"No. What happened to her?" Niki asks.

Baba gets up and moves to her rocking chair. "She was a little girl with black eyes who liked to chatter, much like the cuckoo does. She was also constantly arguing with her brother. One day, their mother got tired of listening to them fighting."

"Did she punish them?" Niki slides closer to Rada.

"Worse," Baba says. "She cursed them to keep them apart. She turned the girl into a cuckoo, who flies around the forest during the day looking for her brother. But the mother turned the boy into an owl, who comes out only at night. The two of them never saw each other again, and the mother lived the rest of her life in peaceful quiet."

"I'd be sad if I couldn't see Rada again," Niki says.

"I'm not so sure I agree." Rada taps Niki on the shoulder. "Kidding. You're not as bad as some of my friends' brothers."

"The cuckoo's story doesn't end there," Baba says. "She once sang all year long, but her song woke the baby Jesus, making Mary angry. She told the bird it could sing only in the spring. So, now the cuckoo sings until *Eniovden* in June."

"Poor bird," Niki says.

"Did you know the cuckoo doesn't build its own nest?" Rada asks Niki.

"It doesn't? Where does it live?"

Rada shrugs. "In abandoned nests, I guess. The cuckoo even lays eggs in other birds' nests and lets those birds hatch its young."

"That's right," Baba says. "The cuckoo's song not only represents spring's arrival, it's also a song of love."

69

"Not more love stories." Niki groans.

"Our stories are filled with tales about love and marriage," Baba says. "It's part of the cycle of life."

"It's more fun hearing stories about people changing into birds or other animals," Niki says.

"I like all of Baba's stories," Rada says. "Let her tell the rest of it."

Baba rocks in her chair. "The cuckoo represents a lonely woman, sometimes one who never married or even someone widowed like me." Baba pauses, then continues. "The bird sings promises about love and meeting your future husband. I once heard the cuckoo singing in an oak tree when I was young. After the bird flew away, I broke a twig off the tree so her promises would come true."

"How can a twig do that?" Rada asks.

"The cuckoo blesses trees it perches on. Their branches have power to attract love."

"It must have worked." Rada smiles. "You found Daydo."

"Yes, but I also removed my scarf from my head and tied a knot in it to be doubly sure to find love."

"Why did you do that?" Niki asks.

"If I found a hair inside when I untied it in three days, it meant I would marry that year. I met your grandfather soon after that, and we did get married right away."

Rada gets up and kisses her grandmother's cheek. "I'm glad you did, or Niki and I wouldn't be here."

### The Swallow's Tale

"Another bird with a sad story is the swallow. She was also once a young maiden," Baba says.

"Did she have an annoying brother, too?" Rada glances at Niki after she returns to the couch.

"No," Baba replies. "She was a shy bride who didn't speak in front of her husband or in-laws."

"A bride isn't supposed to speak to her mother-in-law until *Todorovden*," Rada comments. "Out of respect."

"The custom at that time was to remain silent for forty days, but this bride was silent for three years," Baba says.

"Rada wouldn't be able to do that." Niki laughs.

Rada glares at him, then looks back at her grandmother. "What happened?"

"The man's parents thought something was wrong with the woman. They decided to find a new bride for him," Baba continues. "When he came home that evening with his new wife, his first one met them and finally spoke. 'I've been silent all these years and have never complained about anything. Let this new bride take care of her husband. God, turn me into a bird so I can fly above this house and see if she pampers him.' Her voice soared up the chimney to heaven, and God honored her request. As she started to change, her husband grabbed her by her two braids. They turned into a swallow's tail, which has been split ever since that time."

### The Stork's Test

Rada stands and extends her hand to help Baba. "We should get lunch started before Mom and Dad return."

Niki pleads, "Tell me another story, please. About ... a stork."

"Okay," Baba says. "One more."

"Yeah!" Niki leans into the couch cushion.

"I hope this one's about a bad boy," Rada says.

"Close," Baba says. "It's a tale about a man."

"Men are just big boys." Rada grins.

"A devoted pilgrim often traveled to Christ's tomb to worship his Lord," Baba begins.

"See, he's not bad," Niki taunts Rada.

Rada winks. "Just wait and see."

"God wanted to test how strong the man's faith was," Baba says. "He tied a huge chest to the man's back and told him to climb the tallest mountain. The man asked God, 'What's inside?' God told him to keep it closed and wait on the mountaintop. The journey was long and difficult. The man stopped to rest often and removed the chest from his aching back."

"I don't think I'd like that test." Niki wiggles on the couch, stretching his own back.

"Shh," Rada says. "Let Baba finish."

"Finally the man was too exhausted to go on. 'I'll never reach the top. Maybe if I remove a few things, my trip will be easier.' He undid the latch, then hesitated. God had forbidden him from opening it. His curiosity overcame his desire to do God's will. He wanted to know what weighed the chest down so much. Slowly he lifted the lid."

Niki and Rada both lean closer when Baba pauses.

"Do you know what he found inside?" Baba asks.

"What?" Niki and Rada say.

"Lizards, snakes, and toads swarmed out of the chest, scurrying in all directions." Baba wiggles her fingers to indicate the fleeing creatures. "The man tried to catch them and stuff them back into the chest, but they were too fast and most had disappeared."

"Terrible." Rada shudders. "He should have left the chest shut."

"I bet God was mad when he found out," Niki adds.

"He certainly was," Baba says. "He turned the man into a stork. 'You'll become human again when you return all the creatures to the chest.' Every summer since then, the stork flies around rivers and swamps searching for snakes, lizards, and frogs. It's a hopeless task. When autumn arrives, he leaves that task and travels to Christ's tomb, where he prays that God will forgive him for the sin of disobeying."

"No wonder we have to chase them away now." Rada rises and helps Baba from the rocker.

## *Did you know...?*

*If a stork or swallow builds a nest on the rooftop or in the eaves of your house, it will be protected from misfortune and black magic.*

**Eating Green**

Niki follows his sister and grandmother into the kitchen. Rada removes green leaves from the refrigerator. "Niki, will you get onions and garlic from the pantry?"

"Sure, what are you making for lunch?"

"Nettle soup."

He looks at the nettles while Rada fills the bowl with water. "Are these the prickly kind?"

"Yes, but they won't sting after I cook them."

"I don't like them. Can I have *katmi* instead?"

"No. You had that already for breakfast. We'll have *rybnik*, too."

"Like on my name day! Yum. I love fish and rice." He pokes his finger in the dough that Baba kneads before she wraps it around a carp that's stuffed with rice, raisins, and walnuts.

"You have to eat something green today." Baba hands him a bowl of fruit. "Have a pear for now."

"Okay." He munches on the fruit. "Why do we have to eat something green?"

"In spring everything should be new," Baba replies. "Even the blood running through your veins. Green vegetables are healthy and build up your blood."

"And keep you protected from snakes," Niki adds before he skips off to play.

# Lazarovden

**\*April 23 – Лазаровден – Lazarovden or Lazaritsa: St. Lazarus' Day.**
Eight days before Easter, marking the end of the Orthodox Lent.
*Festival in honor of St. Lazarus, the brother of Mary and Martha. Jesus raised him from the dead after he had been in his tomb for four days.*
*\*A moveable holiday that depends on when Easter is celebrated.*

**St. Lazarus**

The celebrations on ***Lazarovden*** are less about St. Lazarus than about girls proclaiming they're old enough to fall in love and get married. These girls, called *lazarki*, dress in colorful folk costumes or bridal gowns and adorn their hair with jewelry, coins, flowers, and feathers. The Lenten ban on dancing is temporarily lifted. Led by the *kumitsa*, a girl respected by everyone, the *lazarki* sing and dance from house to house. The songs, sung without the accompaniment of instruments, are specially selected for each person. The favorite songs proclaim love and marriage, while others touch on health, prosperity, and fertility.

## ~ ORIGINS ~

In folklore, Lazarus championed goodness. He personified the boundary between life in this world and that in the next.[11] Therefore, *Lazarovden* celebrates nature's revival as it changes from winter's deathlike state.

Celebrations originated from ancient pre-wedding initiation rites for girls that ensured harmony between Earth and the cosmos. The rituals brought happiness to the village and a joyful marriage to newlyweds. Much like the *koledari* ceremonies boys performed in winter on *Survaki*, girls at one time were forbidden to marry if they didn't participate in these springtime rituals. By making their costumes, from spinning the wool, to sewing it together, to adding the proper bridal decorations, girls demonstrated they were adults, because they had the skills needed to take care of their own homes and children.

The girls sang songs in honor of Lada, the goddess of love and family. At the end of the day, they performed a dance for single men and their future mothers-in-law. The men chose brides from among the *lazarki*. Participation in the day's ceremonies also protected the girls from being abducted by the *zmei*, a male dragon.

## Did you know...?

*Wearing a wreath of herbs or bathing in a mixture of herbs, such as sprint gentian, white melilo, and hellebore, can protect you from dragons because the creatures fear these herbs.*

---

[11] Bezovska, Albena and Konstantinova, Daniela (trans.), "Lazaritsa and Tsvetnisa," April 12, 2014, https://bnr.bg/en/post/100385512/lazaritsa-and-tsvetnisa.

## ~ RITUALS IN PRACTICE ~

Twenty village girls, ages ten to eighteen, gather in front of the fireplace at Rada's house after sunrise. They practice ritual dances, recite well wishes, and sing love songs from a selection they chose after *Sirni Zagovezni*. By participating in the day's festivities, the girls, *lazarki*, celebrate their journey into womanhood.

"*Lazarki.*" Rada raps on the countertop to quiet them. "Let's get dressed now. I think we're ready."

"Yes, oh great *kumitsa*," Helena taunts as she bows in mock homage. "We'll follow you from house to house. After all, you *are* the most respected girl in the village."

Rada frowns and points a finger at Helena. "Watch it, or I won't let you lead the younger girls through the fields to honor St. Lazarus."

Helena huffs. "You only got to be leader because your father makes such popular wine." She stomps away to change into her festive bridal clothing and decorate her hair.

# *Lazarki* Attire Symbolism

*The clothing and accessories* lazarki *put on have as much power for protection and fertility as the rituals the girls perform.*

- **Embroidered Shirt** – *Linen is associated with the sky. The numerous threads protect against wickedness on Earth, acting as a secure passage to heaven.*
- **Dress** – *Wool represents the land, the external world, and its power of fertility.*
- **Apron** – *This garment signifies the womb, demonstrating the girl has reached sexual maturity. The embroidery, coins, braids, lace, beads, bells, and other items decorating it also indicate her social status.*
- **Hair adornments** – *These are symbols of the soul. As a sign she's ready for marriage, a girl doesn't wear a shawl over her head. She braids her hair with multiple plaits. Flowers, feathers, tassels, beads, coins and other ornaments adorning her hair act as a sign of strength. People believed uncovered hair attracted the evil eye, but bright adornments transferred attention away from the hair.*
- **Belt** – *This item is a sign of moral purity to indicate that a woman is ready to have children. It demonstrates past, presence, and future—the circle of life in the same way it circles the body. The longer the belt is, the longer a person's life expectancy.*
- **Shoes** – *A bride receives shoes from the groom's family, showing his "possession" of her and any children she'll bear.*[12]

---

[12] Ganeva, Dr. Radoslava. "Bulgarian Folk Costumes – Symbols and Traditions." *Bulgarian Diplomatic Review,* Supplement to Issue 3/2003, Year 3.

Silvia, Helena's younger sister, whispers to Rada. "She's upset that Simeon likes you, and not her."

Rada blushes and goes to her room remembering the festivities on *Sirni Zagovezni*. Simeon was one of three boys who shot flaming arrows at her house. Helena didn't collect any that night.

Rada shakes her head to clear the thought away. She slips on and buttons her long, white linen shirt. Some of the girls borrowed their wedding attire, but Rada made hers. Flowers and other traditional symbols embroidered in red travel up the sleeves and along the neckline. Over the shirt she pulls on a black woolen tunic-style dress, also embroidered along the hem, sleeves, and neckline.

She ties an apron around her waist, the attached bells and coins clinking. Next, she wraps a long belt around her waist; the tassels sway with her movement. She tucks several scarfs over the apron, before she embellishes her outfit with many other accessories, long, dangling earrings, several bracelets and beaded necklaces.

After pulling on leggings, she slips her feet into white, soft leather shoes reaching up to her knees. All that remains is for one of the other girls to braid and adorn her long hair with multi-colored yarn, coins, feathers, and most importantly a flower headdress.

## *Did you know...?*

*The white, red, and black colors of traditional Bulgarian clothing represent the marriage of the gods of creation: the sky (white, male) and the earth (red, female). Together, they form a bond which can defeat the destruction of the earth (represented by the color black), and restore fertility to the land.* [13]

When everyone's dressed, Rada says, "Silvia, are you ready to perform the *laduvane*?"

"Yes," the girl replies. "Let's sing to the rings."

The previous night, the girls had gone to the village well and drawn water with a new, white kettle. Each girl dropped a piece of jewelry into it while singing, "Oh Lada, Lada, I am no longer a young girl." They sprinkled oats into the pot. Without speaking, they brought the "silent water" back to Rada's house, letting its magical powers seep into the rings and oats. Silvia covered the kettle with a red bridal veil and placed it under a rose bush. Now, Silvia is ready to remove each ring and predict its owner's future.

The girls gather in a circle around Silvia and sing short songs, *ladanka*, about courtship, marriage, happiness, and love. Silvia uncovers the kettle, reaches in, and pulls out the first piece of jewelry, a bracelet. A song about lifelong happiness ends as she makes a prediction, "Pavel within a year." Everyone looks to see whose jewelry it is. A girl yells in delight, grabs her token, and scoops up some oats to place under her pillow that night.

"I hope you dream about Pavel," Helena says, "then he'll be certain to become your husband."

The ritual continues. The girls sing about marriage when Silvia retrieves the next ring. She holds up Helena's ring and predicts, "Simeon soon." Helena gives Rada a smug look and retrieves her ring and some oats. As Helena returns to her spot, Silvia winks at Rada.

At last Silvia pulls Rada's ring during a song of eternal love. Silvia says, "A stranger from a distant land." All the girls "Oooh" and look with envy at Rada. Her heart beats fast from the mystery prediction.

To avert attention from herself, Rada turns to Helena. "Please get the young girls together and take them to the fields and forest."

---

[13] Ibid.

Helena walks away, calling, "Come with me. Let's bless our village lands in honor of St. Lazarus, master of land and woods. Stay together so the *zmei* doesn't catch you." The girls younger than thirteen form a tight group and follow her, performing a chain dance and singing songs about abundant harvests and fertility of the land.

## Did you know...?

*Flashes of lightning, shooting stars, large clouds, and rainbows are ways dragons reveal their presence.*

Rada gathers the remaining girls, who dance toward the village center, singing love songs. The first house they stop at belongs to a former *kumitsa*, recently married. While the girls remain in the yard blessing the newlyweds and singing songs about the woman's beauty, Rada covers her right shoulder with a scarf, and approaches the house where the owner waits by the open door.

"Thank you for your blessings." The woman hands Rada several unpainted eggs, symbolic of new life. The girls will dye them the following Thursday, so they're ready for Easter.

The *lazarki* dance their way to each house, singing songs appropriate for the family. For farmers, they sing about abundant harvests. The beekeepers are blessed with songs that encourage the beehives to grow. They sing songs about a mother's pure love for the woman with many children. While dancing along the street, they wish health to anyone they pass. They say silent prayers at the house of a family who has had a recent death. The girls won't sing to them until next year. In return for every home they visit, the girls receive more gifts: eggs, cheese, flour, nuts, dried fruit, and coins.

After they've visited each home, they return to the village center, creating a symbolic circle. They sing a song to Lazarus. "Go away, Lazarus, but come again next year, and then you'll find me as a bride already."

## Did you know...?

*A woman saves her long, white wedding shirt, which is richly embroidered in red, so she can wear it in heaven. Her husband and family will recognize her by the designs on this shirt.*

Rada and Helena meet up at the end of the day. The unmarried young men, Simeon, Pavel, and others, along with their mothers, gather in the village center. All the girls perform a Lazar dance for their audience. Helena looks in Simeon's direction as she twirls around. She smiles and receives his appreciative glance in return.

# Dragons: *Lamia* and *Zmei*

*Bulgarian folklore is filled with tales about dragons who lived in caves, holes, or cracks in rocks. They often appeared with characteristics of other creatures: snakes, fish, birds, and even humans. People once thought serpents or carp turned into dragons if humans didn't see them for forty years.*

*Not all dragons are alike, however. The* la-lamia, *or female dragon, is what we typically consider a dragon, a huge lizard-like creature covered in scales with wings and sharp claws. Some had three, seven, or nine heads. The male of the species, a* zmei, *was often depicted as a human with wings.*

*While the female* lamia *is always dangerous and malicious, the male* zmei *was often kind. He fought against the* lamia *when she appeared as a storm or hail to destroy crops. His great love for a maiden often led him to abduct her. He first tried to entice her to marry him, telling her of the riches she'd have. Only after persuasion failed did the* zmei *resort to snatching a maiden from a* horo *dance.*

*The dragon's marriage to a human always met with misfortune. The bride suffered depression and was ostracized from the community. In one tale, a girl married a dragon she met at his well. After a few years, she wanted to visit her family. Unfortunately, she'd grown a dragon's tail. Wanting to appear normal to her family, she tried to bite the tail off. While at the dragon's well, she heard the songs of friends she had once known, and she frantically chewed at the tail. She died when her heart burst with the effort. The girls buried her by the well. Every year thereafter they performed a* buenetz *dance, not the traditional circle* horo *dance. In the* buenetz, *they dance in a snakelike fashion in honor of the dragon maiden.*

# Tsvetnitsa

**\*April 24 – Цветница – Tsvetnitsa: Flower Day.**
**Връбница – Vrabnitsa: Willow Day or Palm Sunday.**
<u>Sunday, a week before Easter.</u>
*This is the day Jesus rode into Jerusalem on a donkey, while people proclaimed him king. Girls continue performing rites signifying their adulthood.*
*\*A moveable holiday that depends on when Easter is celebrated.*

***Tsvetnitsa*** marks the beginning of Passion or Holy Week, the week before *Velikden*, Easter. Lent for the Orthodox may have ended, but fasting continues until Easter. People go to church to get willow branches, which are more readily available than palm leaves. Willows not only symbolize mourning and sorrow, but also Christ's continued presence among his followers. After the priest blesses the branches, people twist them into wreaths to decorate icons and the thresholds of their homes.

In some parts of Bulgaria, girls perform the *lazaruvane* on this day instead of the previous one. This is also a day filled with flowers as the *lazarki* continue their marriage games and celebrations.

## The Meanings of Flowers

*Flowers have many meanings in Bulgarian culture and folklore.*
- **Lilac and pear**: *Offer protection from unfortunate encounters.*
- **Cherry**: *Attracts a person's loved one.*
- **Red flower**: *Discourages negativity and provides protection from the evil eye.*
- **Red peony** *(symbolic of virginity and beauty): Protects from the evil eye, spells, and Samodivi; wearing one ensures health and long life.*
- **Primrose** *(symbolic of purity, spring, and young love): Red like the sun, it brings joy and warmth. Woven into wreaths, they possess magical powers.*
- **Geranium**: *Protects against the evil eye; brings health and strength.*
- **Wild violet**: *Heals and soothes people and purifies blood to bestow harmony.*[14]

---

[14] Popova, Vyara (trans.), "Tsvetnitsa or the Day of Flowers," April 18, 2011, https://bnr.bg/en/post/100120950/tsvetnitsa-or-the-day-of-flowers.

## ~ ORIGINS ~

These rituals continue to be rites of spring and a girl's transition into womanhood. In addition, the palm or willow also plays a part in the celebrations. The palm leaf was holy in the ancient world. It symbolized spiritual excellence for people who walked righteous paths and died as martyrs. Palm leaves decorated their graves as a sign of their triumph over wickedness. Palm leaves also represented military distinction. Even before people laid them in Jesus' path as he entered Jerusalem, Romans tossed them in front of soldiers who passed in triumphal processions.

## ~ RITUALS IN PRACTICE ~

Rada and the *lazarki* finish twisting willows and flowers into wreaths and place them on their heads. After they exit the house, Rada tacks a willow wreath to the front door. The priest blessed the willows in the church service earlier in the day, so the wreath will ensure her family's health.

Dressed once again in the costumes they wore on *Lazarovden*, the girls proceed to the river to perform the *kumichane*. Helena catches up to Rada and nudges her in the side. "I'm going to win the wreath race today."

"You think so?" Rada arches her brows. "What's your hurry? You want to be first to get married?"

Helena looks around, then whispers. "Yesterday, Simeon told me I was beautiful, and he was sorry he didn't shoot an arrow in my yard. He said he loves me. He even gave me a bunch of basil his grandmother grew out of a snake's head."

Rada stops and grasps Helena's hands. "That's wonderful. That means he wants you to fall madly in love with him. He's a good person. He works hard at farming and will be able to support you if you do get married."

Rada and Helena laugh as they rush to catch up to the other girls who are almost at the river.

The girls line up along the bridge, looking for a spot where the water moves quickest. Rada and Helena find their own places. Rada removes her floral wreath and yells, "Now!"

All the girls toss their wreaths into the river. They watch as they swirl in the eddies. Some wreaths get stuck on rocks, and others sink amidst groans from their owners.

"Go! Go!" Helena shouts when her wreath nears the finish line. It crosses first before four others, and she twirls around. "I won!" She glances toward the group of boys eyeing the girls.

Simeon tips his hat and smiles.

"Come to my house for sweets, everyone." Helena grabs hold of Rada's arm, and they walk together. Helena talks non-stop about Simeon.

Rada laughs when Helena finally stops long enough to take a breath. "It's a good thing you won. If someone else had, I don't think you'd have been able to keep the tradition of not speaking in front of the *kumitsa* until Easter."

"That's a silly custom," Helena says.

"It's a sign of respect," Rada replies. "If you want to get married, you'll have to perform the ritual silence. Remember, you won't be able to speak in front of your mother-in-law until *Todorovden*. And even then, you'll have to bow before her three times."

"We'll see." Helena pulls Rada along. "At least now I can say anything I want to you, and you can't respond any more until Easter, when you bring me eggs you've dyed."

# Velikden

**\*May 1 – Великден – Velikden: Easter or Great Day.**
*The celebration of the resurrection of Christ after his crucifixion. Before Easter was a Christian holiday, the season was celebrated as the rebirth of nature.*
*\*A moveable holiday.*

For some, Easter is about chocolate bunnies, baskets filled with jelly beans, and searching for hidden eggs. Bulgarians, as well as others who celebrate Easter, enjoy those things, too. People believe that even *Samodivi* love Easter, although not as a Christian holiday, but more from its ancient origins. Legends say they punish people who don't celebrate the holiday.

More importantly, Easter, or ***Velikden***, is one of the most holy days in the Christian religion. Without the resurrection, Christianity would not have flourished.

## ~ ORIGINS ~

Even though the rituals surrounding Easter have pagan origins, Easter itself is not a pagan holiday. It's the celebration of Jesus rising to overcome death after three days in the grave. In the early Church, the day coincided with the Jewish Passover, since Jesus was crucified during this time. However, the date of this holiday is determined by the cycle of the moon, a heavenly body many pagans worshiped. In 325 A.D., the Council of Nicaea decided Easter would always fall on a Sunday, and would not follow the Jewish calendar. However, the Council didn't explicitly say how churches should compute the date. It was several decades before religious leaders accepted that Easter would fall on the first Sunday after the first full moon occurring on or after the vernal equinox.

One of the most common foods on Easter is the egg. For Christians, the red egg symbolizes Christ's blood, but the egg, too, has pagan origins. From ancient times, the egg has been a symbol of birth, resurrection and eternal life—life and death—with a belief that the world was born from the golden egg, that is, the sun. The parts of the egg represent the four elements. The shell is symbolic of earth; the membrane represents air; the liquid is water; and the yellow yoke is the sun and therefore fire.

## Did you know...?

*The first Easter egg should always be red so it has healing and protective powers, and can bring prosperity. A red egg held above a person's head can predict if he is under a curse of the evil eye. If the egg sweats, then someone has cast a spell.*

## ~ RITUALS IN PRACTICE ~

The priest hands candles to everyone at the midnight service. The Pavolvs greet others with "Christ is risen." Their friends reply, "He is risen indeed." Everyone blows out their candles and return home.

While Maria and Baba prepare the spicy rice stuffing and lamb for their noon meal, Rada makes dough for *kozunak*, the Easter bread. "Niki, will you bring me a few red eggs we dyed Thursday?"

"Sure." He goes to the fireplace mantel and reaches for a red egg next to the family's icons.

"No, not that one," Rada says.

"Why?" He twists around, his hand on the egg.

"The first red egg is magical." Rada points to a bowl on the counter. "Get them from there."

"What kind of magic does it have?" Niki asks as he plops the bowl of colored eggs next to Rada.

Maria takes a red egg from the bowl, and rubs it on Niki's cheeks.

"Hey, Mom!"

"That's to keep you healthy." She laughs.

## Did you know...?

*If you wait to color Easter eggs on Friday or Saturday instead of Maudy Thursday, you'll have to dye them without telling anyone so the devil doesn't discover you and destroy their healing powers.*

"That's one of its magic abilities," Rada says. "We're also going to take the one we had from last year and bury it in the field after Dad plows it."

"Can I do that?" Niki asks.

"Sure," Georgi says when he enters the room. "It'll go in the first furrow to make the field fertile."

Rada finishes the dough and sets it aside. "After the dough rises, I'm going to braid the bread. I'll let you decorate it with the eggs, Niki."

"How long's that going to take?"

"At least an hour, maybe more," Rada tells him.

"Okay, but what can I do now?"

"We can egg knock."

"Yeah!" Niki searches through the bowl of red eggs, tapping the ends with his fingers, until he finally chooses one. "I'm ready. Get yours."

Rada selects an egg on top, then sits so she's even with Niki's height. They hold the eggs with the pointed end toward each other, and tap them three times. The tip of Rada's egg cracks.

"I beat you!" Niki squeals. "Last year you beat me."

"Try with Dad next," Rada advises. "Take a new egg if you want."

Niki searches through the bowl again, and pulls out a new egg. He selects one for his father, too. "Dad, you ready?"

Georgi reaches for the egg. "Let's go."

Tap, tap, tap. Georgi's egg cracks.

Niki jumps up and down. "I beat Dad. Now Mom and Baba so I'll be healthiest."

He waits until they finish the meal preparations, and knocks eggs with them. Tap, tap, tap. Tap, tap, tap. Niki's red egg remains whole both times.

"Yeah! I'm the winner!" He runs around the room, then plops next to the dozing puppy. "Mom, when are we going to eat?"

"I'll make you something in a little while. You can have an apple now." She gets the fruit and brings it to him. Niki's eyes are closed and his breathing steady. "Georgi?" Maria points to their son.

Georgi picks up the sleeping boy and brings him to bed.

# Coloring Easter Eggs

*White or brown eggs*
*Onion skins*
*Candle*
*Empty plastic vitamin bottles*

*Small paint brush used for art*
*Spaghetti strainer*
*Coffee mugs*

During my childhood, my grandmother colored eggs for Easter with dye made from natural products like onion skins and walnut tree leaves. Today, many people use commercial dyes, but in some villages in Bulgaria people still use natural colors and beeswax candles to decorate Easter eggs. The following describes how to decorate using the traditional methods. As you cook, save several of the dry, outer layers from onions. This may take a while depending on how often you use onions.

**Preparation Steps**

➤ Boil the eggs for 10 - 20 minutes, depending on the size (small to extra large). To prevent cracking, set the heat low, then remove the eggs gently with a spoon.
➤ Put about 6 cups of water and onion skins into a pan. Make sure the skins are covered with water. Bring the liquid to a boil, then simmer for about 20 - 30 minutes.
➤ Light a candle. One made of bees wax is the best.
➤ Set the eggs on the top of empty vitamin bottles.

**Decorate the Eggs**

➤ When the wax has melted, dip a thin paintbrush into it and paint a pattern on the eggs. First paint one half of the egg, let the wax dry, then turn the egg upside down and paint the other half. You can decorate several eggs at the same time if you have multiple bottles to use as stands.
➤ While waiting for the wax pattern to dry, put the pan containing the onion-skin dye back on the stove and bring to a second boil. Using a strainer, pour the dye into coffee mugs, filling them halfway.
➤ Put each egg in a mug and leave it there until the dye cools down, about 20 - 30 minutes.
➤ Pieces of the melted wax will float on the surface. Carefully remove the eggs with a spoon and wipe off the excess wax with a tissue.
➤ Remove the floating wax with a strainer, pour the liquid back into the pan, and boil again. Repeat the above steps to finish the rest of the eggs.

*Continues on next page.*

# Coloring Easter Eggs

Various traditional designs include plants, animals, insects, reptiles, geometric shapes, a stairway of life spiraling to the top of the egg, butterflies (symbol of the soul and resurrection), and vines. A few natural resources used for various dyes include:

Walnut leaves, turmeric (yellow)
Onion peel (yellow or orange)
Apple peels (yellow or light green)
Paprika, oregano, beetroot (red)
Coffee (brown)
Nettles, spinach, clover, parsley (green)
Cabbage juice (lilac)
Blueberries (purple)
Cornflower (blue)
Sumac (orange)

**Modern-Style Alternatives**: Use any color medium-point permanent marker to make designs on the eggs. Another organic way to color them is with decorative paper napkins. My favorite design is daisies. Carefully cover the egg with uncooked egg white like glue. Cut out the pattern from the napkin and paste the design on top. Repeat until you have all the eggs decorated. Let them dry.

Now you are ready to celebrate and have eggs fitting the holiday.
*Hristos Voskrese* and *Voistnie Voskrese* as Bulgarians say on Easter.

# SPRING: What Have You learned?

1. Which of the following do men NOT do on Kukerovden?
   A. Dress in furry costumes and scary masks.
   B. Sing the opera.
   C. Pretend to be a bride and groom.
   D. Perform skits about the harvest.

2. What activity is the highlight of Baba Marta Den?
   A. Playing hop scotch.
   B. Flying paper airplanes.
   C. Sledding down steep hills.
   D. Giving friends bracelets made with red and white yarn.

3. What is NOT mentioned on Blagovets?
   A. Cuckoos, swallows, and storks.
   B. Snakes and lizards.
   C. Little Red Riding Hood and the Hulk.
   D. *Samodivi.*

4. What is something that is NOT true about Samodivi?
   A. They are ugly.
   B. They love to sing and dance.
   C. They have blue eyes.
   D. They live in caves.

5. What game is NOT played on Sirni Zagovezni?
   A. Jumping over bonfires.
   B. Catching a treat with teeth.
   C. Shooting flaming arrows.
   D. Roller skating.

Answers: 1-B; 2-D; 3-C; 4-A; 5-D.

# Summer Rituals

# Kostadinovden

**May 21 – Костадиновден – Kostadinovden: Day of Saints Constantine and Helena.**
**Нестинарство – Nestinarstvo: Fire dancing.**
**Нестинар / Нестинарка – Nestinar (male) / nestinarka (female): Lead fire dancer.**
**Нестинари / Нестинарки – Nestinari (male) / Nestinarki (female): Fire dancers.**
*A day to honor St. Constantine, credited with making Christianity the dominant religion of the Roman Empire, and Helena, his mother, who first taught him this religion. This ritual was originally celebrated on June 3 according to the Julian calendar.*

*The Thracian word* nestia *means "fire." Some say* nestinari *originates from the Bulgarian word* nistina *or* istina *(truth), since the dancers were true Christian believers. Others say that* Nestinarstvo *comes from the Greek words for fasting (*nisteía*) and fire (*estia*).*

**St. Constantine**

Fire dancing, or *Nestinarstvo*, where people walk on live coals with their bare feet, is the highlight of the **Kostadinovden** celebration. Many non-believers call the ritual fake. "People don't really walk on live coals," they say. Or, "The dancers must put an ointment on their feet." Or even something more scientific: "Coals don't conduct enough heat to burn feet as you walk across them." Whatever you choose to believe, the ritual is mystical and awe-inspiring.

Picture the scene unfolding in a village square. A crowd mills around a circle of hot coals. Someone beats a *tupan* (drum), another person plays a *kaval* (shepherd's pipe), while a third musician plays a *gaida* (bagpipe). The sound is eerie, like the prelude to a major event about to happen in a movie. Everyone quiets as a woman in a long, white robe holds an icon of St. Constantine above her head. She steps onto red coals amidst gasps from onlookers. In a trance-like state she dances across the embers and feels no pain, nor does she even get burned.

## ~ ORIGINS ~

Like so many Bulgarian customs, *Nestinarstvo* embraces both Orthodox and pagan beliefs. Some texts say Thracians originally performed the ritual in honor of the Great Mother Goddess Bendis and her offspring, Sabazios, the Sun god. Christianity embraced the ritual when Emperor Constantine I ruled the Roman Empire. He himself worshiped fire, so he allowed the *nestinari* to perform their rites even after he legalized Christianity. The ritual is therefore celebrated on the feast day honoring him and his mother, Helena, transferring it from worship of a pagan mother and son to Christian ones.

The ritual has not always fared well. Over time, the Orthodox Church has persecuted the dancers because of the ritual's pagan origins, and the Communists have oppressed them because of the ritual's religious associations. Continued attacks drove the *nestinari* into remote villages, such as Balgari, Kosti, and Brodilovo in the Strandzha Mountains in southeastern Bulgaria. Researchers assume it was deep within these mountains where *Nestinarstvo* originated. Thracians living in these regions were sun worshipers with strict laws governing their rituals. The remoteness of these villages and the rigid form of worship may be what enabled the custom to continue, presumably unchanged much from its beginnings.

In the time of the Thracians, priestesses performed the ceremony. Today both men and women participate, and either a man or a woman can be the lead dancer. This person chooses his replacement when he can no longer perform the ritual. Often the successor is a son or daughter, since people believe the parent passes on to his child not only the skill to walk on coals, but more importantly, the ability to predict the future.[15]

**Understanding *Nestinarstvo***

The *Nestinarstvo* celebration is part of what is called a *panagyr*, rites honoring particular saints, done to ensure health and fertility, not only for people, but also for animals and land. Those present form three or nine circles around the area where the dancers perform the ritual. These circles are associated with the Sun, the "Fire of Heaven."

Both fire and water are associated with the ritual. Fire has protective properties and increases the Sun's divine power, while water has the capacity to heal. The dancers claim that while they are in a trance, the coals look as if they're covered with water.

Sacrifices were a part of all ancient rituals to the gods. Today, the *kurban*, or sacrificial animal, is slaughtered in reverence to St. Constantine. In the past, up to twenty bulls were sacrificed; now only a few animals are slaughtered. It was said that St. Constantine did not want meat, but blood to make him strong.

Magical aspects of the ceremony have also survived. In ancient times, the *nestinari* were leaders of the village. While they were in a trance, they contacted their ancestors, then made predictions and performed healings. Nowadays, *nestinari* claim reverence to the saints gives them protective power so they can dance on embers without injuring themselves. Once they have entered a trance or *prihvashtane* (possession), they feel pulled toward the fire with all their senses. The outside world disappears as they communicate with the saints. They believe Saint Constantine embodies himself not only within the *nestinari*, but also within the instruments and music, much like a pagan belief that the gods could reincarnate themselves in sound and instruments.[16]

Music played an important role in the *Nestinarstvo* in antiquity, as well as today. Many people have written about the healing and influential power of music. This is evident as early as stories of Orpheus playing his lyre to charm beasts, and David calming Saul.

## *Did you know...?*

*In 2009, UNESCO added* Nestinarstvo *to its World Heritage List. Inclusion on this prestigious list means UNESCO makes money available to promote this unique custom, ensuring its preservation for future generations.*

## ~ RITUALS IN PRACTICE ~

Stars fill the moonless sky. Maria and Georgi pack suitcases for the family's overnight stay in Balgari with an old friend of Baba's. They're traveling to the village to watch the *Nestinarstvo* celebration.

A sleepy-eyed Rada asks, "Why can't we watch it closer to home the way we normally do?"

"Those are done for tourists." Maria removes snacks from the refrigerator and places them into a bag for the trip. "Your father and I decided you and Niki should see a more traditional ceremony this year."

---

[15] Popova, Vyara (trans.), "Nestinarstvo or Bulgarian fire-dancing," May 30, 2011, http://bnr.bg/en/post/100122668/nestinarstvo-or-bulgarian-fire-dancing.

[16] Neykova, Ruzha, "Nestinarstvo: On Materials of South-East Bulgaria," p. 5, https://www.academia.edu/5159119/Nestinarstvo_On_Materials_of_South-East_Bulgaria.

Rada drags her feet toward the couch and sits next to Niki, who's lightly snoring.

## St. Constantine Braves the Fire

Baba looks up from her rocker. "Would you like me to tell you a story about St. Constantine and the *Nestinarstvo* while you wait?"

"Yes, that might keep me awake." Rada yawns. "You're not coming with us?"

"No. My days of traveling are over, but send my greetings to Lidiya and Milen."

"I will. I'm sure they'll miss you."

"The fire dance is ancient," Baba says. "Thousands of years old. Our ancestors, the Thracians, danced for Bendis and the Sun. But the Church disapproved, so now we tell different stories."

"You said you have a tale about St. Constantine," Rada prompts when Baba pauses.

"Yes. A popular legend tells how God once looked for an assistant from among unmarried men to help him manage people. He wanted to find a good way to test their loyalty, then an idea came to him."

"The fire dance?" Rada shifts her position on the couch.

"Exactly." Baba smiles. "God built a fire that burned toward the heavens. It burned for a long time. When only glowing embers remained, he said whoever walked on the coals with his bare feet would be his assistant."

"I'm sure that scared a lot of them away." Rada shivers. "I wouldn't want to burn my feet on the coals."

"You're right," Baba says. "Only one man was brave enough to try. Constantine. He danced across the burning coals unharmed, proving to God his heart was pure."

"Now we honor him today."

"Not only him," Baba adds, "but his mother. Although in this story, Helena is an unmarried woman not related to Constantine."

"What did she do?" Rada leans closer, more awake now.

"After helping for a year with only God as a companion, Constantine was lonely," Baba continues. "He told God he wanted a bride. To make sure the woman was as pure of heart as Constantine, God said she would have to pass the same test and walk on coals."

"And Helena did?"

"Yes. She danced barefoot across the hot embers. From that day, people performed the ritual in honor of them both."

Georgi comes into the room and picks up Niki. "We're ready to leave, Rada. You can sleep on the way. It should be daylight by the time we reach the village."

"Okay." She hugs Baba. "Thanks for the story. I'll tell Niki later if he gets bored."

"We'll be back tomorrow, Mom." Georgi leans to kiss her. "Call Adrian if you need anything."

"I will. Don't worry about me. Enjoy the celebration."

## Dressing the Icons

On their way to the morning church service in Balgari, the Pavlovs, along with Lidiya and Milen, walk past wood stacked inside a circle in the village center.

"Is that where the *nestinari* will dance on fire?" Niki asks.

"Yes," Lidiya answers. "Someone will light it later. By night, it'll have burned down to coals."

The church soon fills with villagers and visitors. Lined up at the front are three icons of the saints: one of St. Constantine, one of St. Helena, and one of the two of them together. The priest performs the liturgy, blessing the icons. At the close of the service, young men pick up the icons and leave before the rest of the congregation.

Outside, Niki looks at the unlit wood. "Where's everyone going?"

Milen says, "They're returning to the *konak*, the saints' chapel, to dress the icons."

"Huh?" Niki cranes his neck to look at Milen. "What do they dress them in?"

"Red silk shirts." Milen winks.

"Milen," Lidiya scolds. "Stop teasing the boy." She gives her husband a playful nudge and positions herself between him and Niki. "The *nestinari* cover the icons with festive red cloths decorated with silver coins and ornaments."

"Sounds fun," Rada says. "Can we watch?"

"Unfortunately, no," Lidiya replies. "It's a secret ceremony they do in complete silence. But, we'll see the icons 'dressed' when the dancers come out of the *konak*."

"While we wait outside, we can listen to the musicians playing the *gaida* and *tupans*," Milen says. "They make a lot of noise."

"Awesome!" Niki catches up to his parents who are a few steps ahead. "I want to learn to play a *gaida*." He positions his hands as if he's playing the bagpipe and makes a shrill noise. "Or maybe a *tupan*." He beats an imaginary drum.

Maria laughs. "I'm not sure Balkan would ever come near you again if you did."

## Messages from the Saint

Everyone waits outside the gate leading to the small, tile-roofed chapel. Soon the dancers emerge holding the decorated icons. One man, carrying a censer filled with fire and incense, sits on a bench and people gather around him.

Rada follows Lidiya with the others. "Who's that?"

"He's the lead *nestinar*. He's spent hours inside the *konak* receiving messages from St. Constantine." She leans closer and whispers, "He's in a trance. Soon he's going to make prophesies. People will ask him specific questions about their future."

The man makes the sign of the cross. When the musicians stop playing, he speaks in a slow, soft voice. "Bless the saint who's spoken to me. Villagers, we must offer a barren cow to St. Constantine to avoid a plague."

"What else does the saint require?" someone from the back shouts.

"To avoid a hailstorm destroying our crops, we have to honor the saint for three days."

A woman holds a young child close to her. "What can you tell me about my son?"

The man looks her way, but stares through her. "All our male children below the age of ten will die if the saint's sacred *ayazmo* isn't repaired."[17]

The villagers murmur among themselves. Some hurry off. Others hold their children closer. Maria looks for Niki and wraps her arm around him. "No need for you to worry," she reassures him. "We're only visitors here. The villagers will make sure the chapel is restored."

The *nestinar* stands, and the musicians play again. He joins the other *nestinari*, and they perform a fast *horo* until they're drenched in sweat. When the dancing stops, everyone turns to face the sun. People kiss the icons, and drop coins into a jar one of the dancers holds.

"They'll use the money for next year's ceremony," Lidiya tells Rada as she drops her own coins into the jar. "And after the predictions, I'm sure some of it will go to restore the *ayazmo*. Everyone's lining up to go there now." She explains who the participants in the procession are. "The priest is first; he's the *epitrope*. The *nestinari* are next. The young men with the icons are after that, then the musicians." She heads toward the people making their way around the *konak*. "Now villagers and guests can join the line."

---

[17] These predictions were taken from Neykova, Ruzha, "Nestinarstvo: On Materials of South-East Bulgaria," https://www.academia.edu/5159119/Nestinarstvo_On_Materials_of_South-East_Bulgaria.

**Blessings and Sacrifice**

The procession dances around the chapel, then proceeds to the sacred spring. Sweet incense from the censer drifts past them as they circle St. Constantine's chapel. Those carrying the icons place them on a wooden bench called an *odar*. The priest sprinkles the images of the saints with holy water from the spring. One of the *nestinari* retrieves candles inside the small enclosure and hands them to the priest. The holy man distributes them to each member of the procession, along with a small vial of holy water, saying, "Blessing and health to you this year."

Rada receives her candle and water. After she lights the candle from a torch, she drops a coin into a basket by the icons. She touches the ornaments hanging on the side of St. Helena's icon. "Bless me, dear saint."

When everyone has received their gifts and made their offerings, the priest speaks. "Now drink water from this sacred spring. May its waters heal you and bring you health."

Lidiya drinks hers, then says, "We can drink the spring water only as part of the ritual. The rest of the year, we have to stay away from the chapel and spring because they're holy and must be kept pure."

A bleating sheep draws their attention toward the priest. He places his hands on the white animal.

"It's customary for the *kurban*, the sacrificial animal, to be a year old," Lidiya says. "There are also a bull and a few more animals that wealthier families have offered for the sacrifice."

"What will they do with all that meat?" Rada asks.

"The *nestinari* get the sheep's shoulder, which they'll share in the *konak* after the *Nestinarstvo*. Then every family in the village will take a piece of the *kurban* home for tonight's meal, and wash it by hand because it's sacred." She pauses. "In olden times, people licked the meat clean of blood."

Rada cringes. "Yuck."

"I'm glad we don't do that any longer," Lidiya says. "Another thing. No one is supposed to take a portion of an animal he brought."

"Does the priest distribute it to everyone?"

"No, but he'll be busy going to every home to bless each *kurban*. Families will give him pieces of the meat and money in return." Lidiya looks toward the priest. "You may not want to watch while he slaughters the sheep."

The priest sprinkles the animal with holy water, turns it toward the east, and lights a candle on its right horn. "Lord, bless this animal, and may its lifeblood protect our village and bring us health."

Rada's face pales, and she turns away when the priest lifts the knife.

The sheep bleats, and people in the crowd gasp. Lidiya takes Rada's hand and leads her toward a meadow where people are dancing and playing games.

**The Fire Dance**

Later in the day when the sun sinks below the mountains, Rada and Lidiya gather in the village square with the growing crowd. They look for Niki and Milen and stand with them.

Niki asks Rada, "Why did you leave the meadow?"

"I wasn't feeling well."

"You missed all kinds of fun games," Niki prattles on. "Dancing. Jumping over fires. And people were hanging upside down from trees, mumbling strange things." He snickers. "I think some others were drunk. They had funny looks in their eyes."

Milen taps him on the shoulder. "Those were *nestinari*. They were still in a trance, not drunk. They should be arriving soon to start the *Nestinarstvo*. See the fire's down to coals now."

Maria and Georgi join them right before the priest leads the parade of musicians and dancers down the street. The dancers wear long-sleeved white shirts. The men have red sashes wrapped around their waists over their black pants. The women wear red embroidered aprons over black sleeveless dresses, and have their heads covered with a white scarf. The crowds cheer the *nestinari* on as they dance around the outskirts of the coals three times. Inside the circle, the lead *nestinar* carefully rakes the still-burning embers, avoiding contact with them. When he's done, he joins the others, and they all dance around the circle once more.

"When are they going to dance barefoot on the coals?" Niki asks Milen.

"Shh. Now. See the lead *nestinar* is holding the icon of St. Constantine above his head."

Lidiya leans closer to Niki after the dancer kisses the icon. "While he's still in a trance, the *nestinar* acts as a mediator between sky and earth. St. Constantine will protect him while he dances across the coals. When he holds the icon, it symbolizes sacrifice and death. It's a way to purify everyone in the village so we can have new life and prosperity."

"Huh?" Niki looks at her.

Lidiya laughs. "I guess that was a lot to take in. Look, he's going into the circle now."

The man holds the icon high as he passes over the coals in graceful steps. The crowd cheers and claps while the music plays. One by one, the *nestinari* cross the coals, holding icons of the saints for protection and reverence. They pass through several times in opposite directions, the sparks from the embers flying around their bare feet as they dance. Every once in a while, the dancers press down on coals in a circular motion. When the music speeds up, so does the dancing.

"The more times the dancers cross the coals, the more prosperous the village will be," Lidiya says.

Finally, after the dancers have extinguished many of the coals, they exit the circle of embers.

"They're not going to crush all of the coal?" Niki asks, disappointed to see some still glowing.

"No," Milen says. "They dance for only about fifteen minutes. In ancient times they crushed all the embers to ashes. It was supposed to burn away misfortune and disease that might come to the village."

"And it gets rid of sin, too," Lidiya adds. "The fire purifies the dancers with its healing powers, and opens a door to the spirit world. They'll make more predictions on their way back to the *konak*."

"Doesn't it hurt at all?" Rada asks.

"No, they're protected," Lidiya says. "Baba Zlata, a former *nestinarka*, once told us about her experience. She said, 'When I sense the sorrow coming, my arms and feet start to feel as if they were wooden. I don't know about the heart, but the feeling in my head is a peculiar one. I see people around, but not very clearly. When the power of fire comes, it all turns into a mist. I circle around the fire, and when I see it strong – I do not enter. When I feel enough power, if St. Constantine gives it, I simply jump inside, feeling absolutely nothing – no pain, no burning! The fire then looks as if it was covered with water, as if it was gold.' "[18]

The dancers join hands and perform a *horo* around the exterior of the coals.

"All the *nestinari* have to participate in the final dance," Lidiya says, "to make sure the entire village will be healthy."

"That was awesome," Niki says when the dancers and musicians disappear down the road. "I want to be a *nestinar*."

"Unfortunately," Lidiya says, "not everyone can perform the dance. You have to be born into a family of *nestinari*. Not everyone in those families becomes a dancer either. It takes a lot of mental preparation to master the art. And the dancers have to be special people who have complete faith in good, and never wish misfortune on anyone."

"I guess that leaves you out, Niki," Rada says. "You're not always good."

"Neither are you." He pouts.

"I'd rather dance the *horo*, than the *Nestinarstvo* anyway," she adds.

---

[18] Stanchev, Zhivko (trans.), "Magic ritual of Nestinarstvo in Strandja," May 31, 2012, http://bnr.bg/en/post/100155800/magic-ritual-of-nestinarstvo-in-strandja.

# Eniovden

> **June 24 – Еньовден – Eniovden: Enio's Day or Midsummer's Day.**
> *The summer solstice, which coincides with the Eastern Orthodox Feast of St. John the Baptist, celebrates his birth six months prior to that of Jesus. John proclaimed a message of repentance as he paved the way for the Savior. Beheaded by King Herod between 31 and 36 A. D. This is also a day where love and herbs play important roles.*

**St. John the Baptist**

*Eniovden* is filled with rituals about love. One tradition, *Eniova Bulia* or Enio's Bride, is based on a tale about an ill-fated love between Stana and Enio. In this ceremony, a girl between the ages of three and five dresses like a bride, complete with red veil. Young women parade the "bride" around the village to each well, spring, field, and garden. At the end, a ritual "bathing" of the bride takes place.

Then the women gather around her while they perform the *laduvane*, the "singing to the rings" ceremony. While they sing love songs about weddings and prosperity, in honor of Lada, the Slavic goddess of love and family, the child bride makes predictions about the future of the women from their rings, which are tied to a bouquet of flowers. The women ask questions about health, marriage, and fertility, and the child predicts which man will love the owner of the ring. This ritual is also often performed on *Survaki*, *Gergiovden*, and *Lazarovden*.

The holiday is about more than love, however. Saint Enio was called the "Herb Gatherer," so the day focuses on herbs as well. On the eve of *Eniovden*, women pick seventy-seven and a half herbs and store them in water. The herbs represent seventy-seven known illnesses and half an herb for unknown ones. A popular belief is the herbs have magical and healing powers if picked on the eve of *Eniovden*. However, the women must remain silent as they pour water over the herbs, so the magic is not ruined by the human voice. They cover the caldron of herbs with an apron and leave it under the stars overnight to make the herbs even more powerful.

Women find many uses for herbs. In one ceremony, they place some on each corner of a field while singing. This ensures a bountiful harvest and prevents witches from stealing the fertility of the land, contained in the dew. Otherwise, witches would cast spells on the fields during the night, collect the dew in their aprons, and bring it to their own fields.

With other magical, healing herbs, women create a giant wreath. Then, dressed in colorful, traditional costumes, they dance the *horo* before they step through the wreath to start the day's celebrations.

*Enivoden* is also a night when the boundaries between the spirit and human worlds merge, allowing creatures from heaven, earth, and the underworld to roam the land. *Samodivi* and dragons celebrate on this day. People wear red threads, like *martenitsi*, on their wrists to ward off danger from these creatures if they happen to run across one in the forest.

Finally, like many other Bulgarian holidays, people perform rituals to ensure health and well-being, such as bathing in the morning dew or checking how well-formed their shadows are.

## ~ ORIGINS ~

In Bulgarian mythology, the Sun (a male deity), along with his twin, the Moon (a female deity), were created when the sky and earth merged. Both light sources played prominent roles in the beliefs of the Thracians, but on the summer solstice, or Midsummer's Day, people worshiped the Sun. While it rose that day, they believed the Sun bathed in the sea, rested a while, then shook itself, covering the land with dew. Refreshed, the Sun continued its exhaustive, upward journey to the highest point in the sky. Joyful at having reached the height of summer, the Sun danced, turning three times before descending, marking the transition toward winter.

People today continue the tradition of watching the sun rise and dance. In times past, and perhaps even today, people believed that any water the sun's rays touched along its way to the top of the sky acquired healing powers. People bathed in it or rolled in dew to ensure their good health.

Acquiring health was not the only important aspect of the day. Thracian kings performed immortality rites on the solstice at a place they considered the gateway to the afterlife. The ceremony included a ritual bath, after which the king passed through a stone arch (the womb of the Great Goddess) as the Sun penetrated it. The ceremony symbolized the marriage between Sun and Earth (a female deity), which brought about the king's conception and re-birth.

## ~ RITUALS IN PRACTICE ~

On the eve of *Eniovden*, Maria ties a red, twisted thread around her wrist. She glances out the window. The sun's light reflects against the Black Sea, making it sparkle. "Rada, I'm going to Sultana's now, while it's still light. I'll help with her garden before we gather herbs."

"Okay," Rada says. "I'll keep Niki out of trouble."

"I'm honored Sultana chose me to learn her healing arts," Maria says. "So many people are afraid of her, but she's always helped us when we've needed anything."

"Maybe someday you'll teach it to me, too. Then I can know how to make Niki stop pestering me."

"Don't fret. When he gets a little older, he'll want to protect his sister." Maria wraps a scarf over her hair. "I'll see you tomorrow morning. We can make wreaths together."

### Healing Herbs

In the forest, Maria stops at the *cheshma* dedicated to the *Samodivi* to leave a jar of honey. She clutches the red thread around her wrist, then hurries the rest of the way to Sultana's cottage before the sun dips below the horizon.

Sultana rocks on the porch. Two empty wicker baskets sit near the door. "Maria, It's so nice to see you." She rises and the two women enter the house. Drying herbs line the walls and fireplace mantel, and jars of others are stacked on a bookcase.

Maria breathes in deeply the scent of geraniums. "I love the aroma of your home."

The women collect tools for the garden and exit through the back door. They till the soil for a few hours, then return. Sultana takes a seat by the fireplace and motions for Maria to sit. "Do you want to help bundle the herbs?"

"Yes." Maria gathers a bunch and twists them together the way Sultana shows her.

They chat while working through the night, hanging herbs to dry until a few hours before dawn.

"I think we should go now." Sultana stands.

Maria finishes her batch and rises. "I have the list of herbs we need to collect. Seventy-seven and a half." She shakes her head. "I always find the 'half' herb amusing."

"We have to account for those unknown ailments somehow. Half an herb seems a good way." Sultana hobbles to the door. "Herbs are magical tonight. They'll have great healing power. Come along. I'll show you where to find all the different ones."

They gather herbs throughout the forest. Maria glances around from time to time.

Sultana smiles. "Don't worry. *Samodivi* won't bother us. You're safe with me."

After they've collected all the herbs, they return to the cottage. Sultana places them in a caldron and fills a kettle with water. The two women remain silent as Sultana pours the liquid over the herbs, then covers the caldron with her apron and hands the container to Maria. "Please put this out by the porch under the rose bush. The magic of the stars will make them more powerful."

Maria places the caldron where Sultana directed, then returns. The two women continue to work, making bouquets of herbs. Sultana explains each one as they perform the task. "Geraniums are good for health and protection from the evil eye. Primrose will bring you joy. Cherry blossoms are used to attract someone you love."

When the light of dawn creeps over the horizon, Sultana rises. "Let's greet the sun now and watch it dance in sky."

Outside, the sun's light flickers through the trees. After a moment of silence, the women roll in the dewy grass.

Maria stands in an open area, facing the sun. "I'm sure I saw the sun dance three times. That should keep me healthy this year." Turning her head, she looks over her shoulder. "Now it's definite. I won't get sick. My shadow's not fuzzy, not even my head."

"That's a good sign," Sultana says.

"Thank you for everything you've taught me today. I hope I can remember it all."

"We have time. Don't worry. I'll teach you everything I know." Sultana picks up the pot of herbs and gives a few to Maria. "You can add these to the magic wreath."

## Magical Wreath and the *Laduvane*

Rada has already made breakfast for the family when Maria returns. The women dress in their festive holiday clothes, and mother and daughter join other women in the village center. They all combine the herbs they collected the night before and make an enormous wreath. After everyone dances a *horo*, two women hold the wreath steady, while each young woman steps through it three times.

"We should all be healthy now," someone says.

"And fertile." Another young woman giggles.

The mother of a five-year old girl brings her daughter to the gathering. "Now, Sophia," the mother says as she straightens her daughter's white dress and adjusts her red jacket, "don't be scared. We're going to take turns carrying you around the village."

"She's so adorable dressed like a bride." Rada leans to lift the child's red veil, moving aside the silver coin attached to it. She makes sure not to knock off the wreath of flowers over the veil. "Hi, I'm Rada. May I be first to carry Enio's Bride?"

The child lowers her head and says, "Yes."

Rada picks up the girl and wraps her arms around the tiny waist. She walks toward the *cheshma*, listening to its water flow into the marble basin. The women sing love songs as they make their way around the village, going to the small *cheshma* dedicated to the *Samodivi*, then through the village to visit everyone's garden, and finally back to the village center where they sprinkle the girl with water from the *cheshma*.

The girl's mother sets a pot in front of her daughter. She ties a scarf around the girl's eyes. "It's time to make the *laduvane* predictions." She guides Sophia's hand to the pot. Inside are bunches of seven, nine, or twelve wildflowers tied with a red thread. Attached to each bouquet is a ring or other ornament belonging to the young, unmarried women. The flowers and jewelry soaked in the water overnight.

Sophia reaches in and removes a bouquet. Similar to the ceremony on *Lazarovden*, the girl predicts marriage and love for each woman present.

**Legend of Eino's Bride**

"You did well," Rada tells Sophia. She hands the girl a doll made from two boards bound together like a cross, its body dressed in a bridal outfit. "Do you know the story of Enio and his bride?"

"A little. Mom told me this morning, but I was too excited to listen. Do you know it?"

"Yes. Would you like me to tell it to you again?"

"Oh, yes, please." Sophia clasps her hands around the gift and looks expectantly at Rada.

Rada sits next to her on the edge of the *cheshma*. "A long time ago, Enio fell in love with a girl named Stana. Every day they thought about each other. They'd say, 'Bread doesn't taste good if we can't see each other.' "

Sophia giggles. "My sister says that when she doesn't see her boyfriend."

"In those days, people couldn't choose the person they wanted to marry."

"Really?" Sophia asks. "Why?"

"They lived off the land, much like many people here still do," Rada says. "They arranged marriages that would help them survive."

"Oh." The girl purses her lips, a confused look on her face. "Did Enio and Stana get married?"

"No. Stana's father didn't like Enio. He found her a husband from another village."

"That's mean."

"Stana thought so, too, but she had to obey her father," Rada says. "On her wedding day, her mother dressed her, braided her hair, and put on a red wedding veil. 'Don't worry, darling. The man you marry will take care of you, like your father has taken care of us.' Stana was sad, but left with the matchmakers who came to bring her to her husband."

"Will Enio stop her?"

"No. He couldn't do anything. His own father sent him to work in the field so he wouldn't cause trouble. It was their custom to never refuse to get married." Rada clears her throat. "Stana sobbed along the way. Tears streaked her cheeks. She didn't want to marry anyone except Enio."

"What's she going to do?" Sophia leans closer.

"They came to a bridge and Stana's grief made her crazy. She tore the veil off and hurled it to the ground. Then she jumped off the bridge into the swollen river."

Sophia gasps. "Did she drown?"

"Yes, and when Enio found out, he was filled with so much pain he became ill. He lay down in bed and stayed there for nine years."

"That's older than I am."

"It is a long time," Rada says. "His sister thought so, too. Enio's grief hurt everyone because all the time he was in bed, it didn't rain. The river where Stana drowned dried up. All the crops withered, and their farm animals died. Without food, people started dying, too."

"Oh no! Enio has to get up to save them." Sophia clutches the doll to her chest.

"His sister thought the only way to do that was to pretend Stana came back for him," Rada continues. "She made a doll like the one I gave you. She tied a piece from a loom and a rolling pin together, and wrapped it up like a bride with a veil. 'Get up, brother. Stana, your bride, is here for you.' Enio opened his eyes, looked at the doll, and smiled. He held out his arms and said, 'Stana, my love.' Then he fell back on the bed and died."

"He died, too?"

"Yes, but he went to be with Stana, and they were happy together. The curse broke when he died. A strong wind blew across the village, and the rain returned. All the fields grew crops again, and animals became healthy." Rada pauses. "All the young girls started singing love songs about Stana and Enio. They made a bride every year to remember the poor girl."

"That's me!" Sophia smiles and hugs her doll.

# Prokopi Pchelar

**July 8 – Прокопи Пчелар – Prokopi Pchelar: Prokopi Beekeeper, Beekeeper's Day.** *Festival in honor of St. Procopius of Scythopolis, the patron of beekeepers. Martyred 303 A.D. He was beheaded after he refused to offer sacrifices to pagan gods or to the emperors. Said to be the first martyr in Palestine.*

**St. Procopius**

In addition to wine production mentioned in the *Trifonovden* rite, another well-known Bulgarian livelihood is beekeeping. It's no wonder the country has a day, actually two, honoring beekeepers. On ***Prokopi Pchelar***, beekeepers perform rituals to entice bees to produce an abundance of honey. They also give away jars of honey and bread coated with the sticky substance as a way to protect family and friends since they believe honey has magical and curative powers.

On February 10 Bulgarians also celebrate *Chouminden*, or Plague Day, in honor of St. Haralambos, patron of beekeepers and protector against illnesses, especially the plague.

## *Did you know...?*

*Honey never spoils. Archaeologists found honey preserved for thousands of years inside pots in Egyptian tombs.*

## ~ ORIGINS ~

According to mythology, the first beekeeper was Aristaeus, son of Apollo and water-nymph Cyrene. Legends credit this demigod with inventing beehives. To collect honey, he wrapped his body with linen as protection from bee stings. He tricked bees into letting him retrieve honey by swinging a torch around until smoke filled the hive. Then he beat metal plates together to drown out the buzzing. The confused creatures didn't bother him as he reached into the hive to gather combs.[19]

While Aristaeus was in Thrace, he met Orpheus's wife Eurydice, and fell in love. She fled from him and stepped on a snake, which bit her heel, killing her. The nymphs punished him by making his bees fatally ill. With the help of his mother, Aristaeus tricked the prophet Proteus into telling him how to regain his bees. He had to appease the nymphs by slaughtering four bulls and four cows, all perfect and beautiful. When he had completed the task, Aristaeus examined the sacrificed animals, discovering a swarm of bees in the carcass of one.[20] This led people in antiquity to believe bees were born from decaying flesh.

### Honey: Food of Gods and Nymphs

Many people know that honey is described as the food of the gods in mythology. In Bulgarian folklore, honey also played an important role as an offering to *Samodivi*. Once such place people made offer-

---

[19] Theoi Greek Mythology, "Aristaios," http://www.theoi.com/Georgikos/Aristaios.html.

[20] Bulfinch, Thomas. Bulfinch's Mythology: The Age of Fable or Stories of Gods and Heroes. Chapter 24. http://www.greekmythology.com/Books/Bulfinch/B_Chapter_24/b_chapter_24.html.

ings was at caves where these nymphs of the forests and waterways lived. Archaeologists have discovered such a cave to nymphs on the isle of Ithaca. Since the end of the Bronze Age, people have placed gifts on a round paved platform by the cave. Inside the cave are reliefs and dedications to nymphs, as well as vessels for drinking and libations.[21]

A passage in Homer's *Odyssey* describes this cave.

*High at the head a branching olive grows*
*And crowns the pointed cliffs with shady boughs.*
*A cavern pleasant, though involved in night,*
*Beneath it lies, the Naiades delight:*
*Where bowls and urns of workmanship divine*
*And massy beams in native marble shine;*
*On which the Nymphs amazing webs display,*
*Of purple hue and exquisite array,*
*The busy bees within the urns secure*
*Honey delicious, and like nectar pure.*
*Perpetual waters through the grotto glide,*
*A lofty gate unfolds on either side;*
*That to the north is pervious to mankind:*
*The sacred south t'immortals is consign'd.*

In the Eastern Rhodope Mountains of Bulgaria, archaeologists have discovered seven formations similar to those in Ithaca. Pits with grooves in the rocks indicate people poured libations for sacrifices there. Archaeologists think these could have been used for ritual ceremonies depicting the creation of the cosmos; others say they were funeral mounds.[22] Perhaps Thracians also honored *Samodivi* in these sites.

People left offerings of honey to other beings, as well, such as the Black Plague. They set honey, bread, and wine on a table to appease this hunchbacked old woman dressed in rags and carrying a scythe or sickle. Her name could not be spoken. Instead, they called her auntie, sweet, or honey. Another way to protect friends and family from the Black Death was to give away bread and honey.

## ~ RITUALS IN PRACTICE ~

A heavy mist hangs over the village in the early-morning hours. Maria places bread decorated with images of beehives into the oven as someone knocks at the door. "Rada, could you see who that is?"

Rada wipes her hands on her apron and opens the door. "Hi, Mrs. Aneva. Come in."

Maria peeks around the corner. "Daniela, I thought you'd be at your beehives already this morning."

"Nona was supposed to go with me, but she's disappeared again, with a jar of honey and some rolls I baked." Daniela sighs and lowers her voice. "Off to give them to the ... *Samodivi* I suppose. Heavens only knows what really happened to Nona when she disappeared as a child." She pauses. "Would you ... come with me to the hives?"

"Certainly." Maria turns to Rada. "Please take the bread out when it's done."

"I normally wouldn't mind going alone, but last night I had a dream about bees landing on dry branches." Daniela shivers. "The bad omen frightened me. Nona's already lost her father. What would become of her if something happened to me, too?"

Maria pats her friend's shoulder. "It's unfortunate you didn't dream the bees were collecting honey."

---

[21] Fol, Valeria, "Rock-Cut Caves with Two Entrances or the Model of the Cosmos," p. 239, In *Thracia* 15, pp. 239 – 250. Sofia: Tangra TanNakRa Publishing House, 2003.

[22] Ibid., p. 241.

"I know. Then I'd be sure to become wealthy."

"I have something." Maria retrieves a blue bead like an eye from a drawer. "This'll protect you."

"Ah, yes, protection from the evil eye. Thank you." She clutches the charm.

## Did you know...?

*Bees are essential for many species of trees and plants to exist. If all bees died, much of our ecosystem would become extinct and our lives would change drastically. Consider a quote attributed to Albert Einstein: "If the bee disappeared from the surface of the earth, man would have no more than four years to live."*

At the beehives, Daniela lights incense and walks among the cone-shaped hives woven from willow branches. "Whoever is happy and does good, let him sit on a thorn so the bees will swarm."

They put on protective gear and Daniela lifts a hive, removing a comb. She smears honey from it onto the ritual loaves of bread, covering the beehive images on top. "One for God. One for St. Procopius."

Maria reaches for the bread. "Let me hold those while you get the rest of the honeycombs."

"It's still exciting to extract the first honey of the season." Daniela retrieves a small amount of honey from each hive and puts it into a bowl.

Finished with collecting honey, the women remove their protective gear. Maria asks, "Would you like me to go with you to the church, too?"

"If you don't mind."

"It's my pleasure."

At the church, the priest blesses the bowl of honey, and Daniela leaves it on a shelf. "I'll come back tomorrow to get it. Maybe this year after I put some on Nona's forehead, its special healing powers will cure whatever's preventing her from speaking."

"I'm sure she'll speak one day, telling us what happened."

"We can hope and pray." Daniela sighs. "Will you and your family join me for the ritual meal this evening?"

"We'd love to."

Daniela hands Maria a loaf of bread. "This has last year's honey. You're like family to me. As the hive keeps the family of bees together, may this keep your family healthy, so you'll all have long lives."

### Blessed Bees

Maria returns home to discover Baba telling her children a story.

"In the ancient world, bees were messengers between our world and heaven. One day God decided to marry the Sun. He invited everyone to the wedding except Satan."

"Yah, he's bad," Niki says. "I wouldn't invite him either."

"Only that made Satan angry, so he came anyway. He joined a group of guests and laughed while pointing at God. This made God curious what Satan was planning. 'Faithful bee, you are light of wing and swift of foot. Please find out what my adversary is saying.' The bee flew away and landed on Satan's hat to listen."

"Rada tells me it isn't nice to eavesdrop," Niki says.

"In this case it's okay, since God told the bee to do it," Rada says. "It's only wrong when you're listening to *my* conversations."

"Do you two want to argue or listen to the story?" Baba taps her fingers against her leg.

"Sorry, we'll be quiet. Right, Niki?"

"Yes, sorry, Baba."

"The bee was shocked at what she heard," Baba continues. "Satan was saying God was stupid to marry the Sun. 'Look how hot it gets in the summer with only one Sun in the sky. If they have children, all those extra Suns will burn everything.' The bee flew to warn God not to marry the Sun. Unfortunately, Satan saw the bee and chased her."

"Oh, no! Does he catch her?" Niki asks.

"No, but he shot an arrow. It hit her in the waist, almost breaking her body in half. Even wounded, the bee made it back to God and told him what she heard. God thanked the courageous bee and called off the wedding."

"Let's hope no bees show up at Helena's wedding on *Dimitrovden*," Rada says.

"I was her age when I got married, but it seems so young now." Baba sighs. "But to finish the story, the bee was ashamed. Not because she was hurt, but because she had been so afraid of Satan she had wet herself. God told her, 'Don't be humiliated. I'll turn your shame into a blessing. The mess you made will turn sweet-smelling and be given to others as a gift.' The bee asked, 'What about my body?' God told her, 'It will remain broken, but you'll always be happy and sing.' And that's how the bee came to make the precious gift of honey."

# Honey for Health and Life

*People eat honey not only because it tastes good, but also because it has healing powers. In the ancient world, it was used to preserve bodies from decaying. Instead of water, people poured honey onto their hands to purify them when they performed sacred rites. They also believed a little honey on the tongue would prevent defilement and misfortune.*

*Today, honey has many medicinal uses, including combining it with cinnamon to fight the common cold. Besides honey-glazed bread accompanying ceremonies from birth, to marriage, to death, honey also plays a part in major Bulgarian life events.*

- *During a baby's first ritual bath, the mother and grandmother chant, "May you buzz like a bee and be sweet like honey."*

- *A bride smears honey and butter over the threshold of her new house before she enters. Inside, her mother-in-law hands her honey and salt to ensure the couple has joy despite any hardships they may encounter.*

- *At gravesites on All Souls' Day, people distribute a simple meal to those they meet as they honor the dead: ritual bread, boiled wheat with walnuts and honey, and wine.*

# SUMMER: What Have You Learned?

1. Which of the following is NOT an ancient ritual people in Bulgaria still perform in the summer?
   - A. Dress a young girl as a bride.
   - B. Toast marshmallows over an outside fire.
   - C. Roll around in the morning dew on the longest day of the year.
   - D. Dance on hot coals with bare feet.

2. What ritual do fire dancers perform in addition to walking on hot coals?
   - A. Listen to the radio to find out what the weather will be.
   - B. Wear heavy shoes so their feet don't burn.
   - C. Go into a trance and make predictions.
   - D. Play songs on an electric guitar.

3. What do people in Bulgaria do on Eniovden?
   - A. Gather 77 1/2 herbs.
   - B. Look over their shoulders to see their shadows.
   - C. Create a giant wreath made of herbs.
   - D. All of the above.

4. What is true about honey?
   - A. It will go bad after a few years.
   - B. Grasshoppers make it.
   - C. It's used in medicines because it heals.
   - D. Samodivi hate it.

Answers: 1-B; 2-C; 3-D; 4-C.

# Fall Rituals

# Dimitrovden

**St. Demetrius**

**October 26 – Димитровден – Dimitrovden: St. Demetrius' Day / St. Dimitar's Day.**
*Festival in honor of St. Demetrius of Thessaloniki, the protector of winter and cold. Patron of soldiers and the crusades. Born 270 A.D. Martyred 306 A.D. He is often dressed as a Roman soldier and seen carrying a spear. Emperor Maximian ordered guards to pierce Demetrius with spears while the saint was in prison for his faith in Christianity.*

**Dimitrovden**, like other Bulgarian holidays, has its share of unique rituals and beliefs, many about forecasting weather, but it's mostly a day set aside to honor the saint. This day is closely linked to another holiday, *Gergiovden*, St. George's Day, which takes place on May 6. The two festivals mark the beginning and ending of the farming season. Since ancient societies divided the calendar into two seasons, *Gergiovden* was associated with the start of summer and *Dimitrovden*, the beginning of winter.

## Did you know...?

*If a full moon falls on* Dimitrovden, *spring will arrive early, and bees will increase and produce an abundance of honey.*

Legends describe the two saints as twins, although unusual ones. George, young and energetic like spring, rides a white horse. In contrast, Demetrius, mounted on a red one, is old with a long, white beard from which snowflakes flow. While St. George is famous for killing a dragon, icons display St. Demetrius thrusting a spear through a gladiator named Lyaeos, who killed many Christians.

These two holidays are only a few of many patron saint festivals that Bulgarians celebrate. The festivities can last up to three days. The day before the official saint holiday, legends say the saint's spirit arrives at the home. The family sets bread (*vechernik*, or evening loaf) for him on a small table (*vechernitsa*, or evening table).

On the actual feast day, women begin preparing the ritual meal early by baking bread and cooking sacrificial meat. Usually they make two types of bread, one for God and one for the saint, which the village priest consecrates. The type of meat they serve varies with the holiday. Poultry is common on *Dimitrovden*, while they serve lamb on *Gergiovden*.

Before the meal begins, the head of household lights incense and walks around the table three times while he blesses the family. During the meal, he breaks the bread, makes the sign of the cross over it, and pours wine onto the bread.

The final festival day is *Pateritsa*, named after the crutch, or magic stick, the saint uses for blessing the family. This is the day the saint departs. Some people say he leaves his crutch for the fellowship offered him, while others say he takes it with him, ready to bring it back to bless the family the following year. To honor the saint, the head of the family breaks the previous day's bread and places half by the saint's icon. He spreads the rest over fields to honor God.[23]

## ~ ORIGINS ~

Agricultural societies rested after the autumn harvest, before they became busy planting again in spring. People set aside food to last them through the long winter. They lit candles in the stables and near produce and wood supplies to keep spirits away.

Long before Christianity became the official religion, after the harvest, communities honored both nature and the *saybia*, the protector of households and livestock. This person was often an influential family member, a priest, or a well-known member of the community. After he died, his spirit remained to guard families and their possessions. People even believed he entered the dreams of the eldest living male to give warnings of danger or misfortune. Once a year, the family gathered to honor the *saybia* with a special meal. With the arrival of Christianity, instead of expressing gratitude to a *saybia* on a single day, people dedicated numerous days to honor many saints.[24]

In ancient times, celebrations to the household's patron spirit often took place at an *obrok*, a holy place people believed righteous spirits frequented. This site was usually located in or near the village, often by a *cheshma* (fountain) or well. Or they might hold it in a glade, protected by branches of centuries-old trees. Oftentimes, it was in a location where stones had been arranged in a semicircle by some unknown person at an even earlier date. People were forbidden to tamper with the trees, rocks, and water because the location was sacred.

### Thracian Horseman

St. George and possibly St. Demetrius have an ancient association with Heros, also called the Thracian Horseman. Some legends describe Heros as a human hero or a lesser deity who acted as a mediator between people and gods. Others say he was a god himself, the son or lover of the goddess Bendis, and he ruled the underworld, bringing life, death, and fertility to land and people. In this respect, Heros could represent both brothers: George, who brought life and fertility in spring, and Demetrius who caused death with winter.

Demetrius was also associated with the underworld and the souls of ancestors. *Dimitrovska Zadushnitsa*, All Soul's Day, falls on the Saturday before *Dimitrovden*.

Most often, images show Heros riding a horse and slaying a beast, much like George slaying the dragon. George's dragon-slaying feats could also have originated from other heroes in Bulgarian legends who fought against the fierce female *lamia*. One such legend is "The Three Brothers and the Golden Apple." In this story, a young man saved a king's daughter before she was eaten by a three-headed dragon. Or George could have been modelled after Krali Marko. This legendary hero released young women and men whom a *lamia* had enslaved.

### Sheep Herding and Wedding Arrangements

Both *Gergiovden* and *Dimitrovden* were originally associated with another Bulgarian occupation: sheep herding. In the spring, on *Gergiovden*, hired men drove sheep to the mountains to graze. While they

---

[23] Bezovska, Albena and Atanasov, Kostadin (trans.). "Details and facts about Bulgarian family services and religious sacrifice." Aug. 31, 2014. http://bnr.bg/en/post/print/100453885/details-and-facts-about-bulgarian-family-services-and-religious-sacrifice.

[24] Ibid.

were gone, women performed rituals for the men's success and protection. It was also a day women sang to their rings as they did on *Eniovden*, and made predictions about whom they would marry.

The entire community gathered to celebrate the men's return on *Dimitrovden*. With the harvest over and the men paid for their labor, the wedding season began. Women old enough to marry performed a *horo*. According to tradition, parents of young men choose brides for their sons from among these women.

The suitor's parents sent friends or close relatives to the chosen woman's home, to discover if her parents would agree to the marriage. The guests didn't speak directly about the purpose of their visit. Instead their words and actions were symbolic. The messengers sat by the hearth and raked coals in the fire with metal tongs called *masha*. This was a sign that they came to discuss the marriage. If the woman's parents didn't like the man who wanted to marry their daughter, or even if they disliked his family, they would say she was too young to be married. If they liked the arrangement between the two young people, they said they would think about it.

The two families held more meetings, and when both sides came to an agreement, they exchanged gifts, sealing the contract. Then a festive ceremony with music and a feast kicked off the engagement period, which lasted only a few weeks. After the engagement, the man and woman could meet publicly during the day, but had to be accompanied by an escort.

Not all marriages were arranged, however. In the county, young people could marry for love. The man's father and some of his relatives went to the woman's house. Her own father would ask her three times if she wanted to marry the youth. If she answered "yes" each time, the couple officially became engaged. The groom's father offered the family a drink from his *baklitsa* filled with wine.

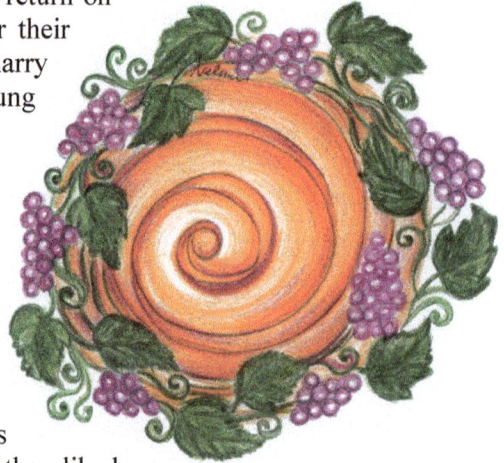

## ~ RITUALS IN PRACTICE ~

The Pavlov family gets ready for Helena and Simeon's *venchavka*, their wedding ceremony. The two became engaged over the summer when Helena turned eighteen. They asked Maria and Georgi to be the *kum* and *kuma*, best man and matron of honor, at the wedding. Delighted at the special honor, they both agreed.

"Rada, please get me the grapevines so I can make the groom's crown." Maria inserts the final rose into the boxwood wound around the bridal wreath. White carnations alternate with red roses and ribbons.

Rada hands the vine to her mother. "I thought you were supposed to make them on Saturday."

"I had to wait for the roses. I wanted them to be fresh today." Maria twists the shoots together. "Did Helena say why she didn't want to use the church's golden crowns?"

"You know her," Rada says. "She believes in traditions and wanted to go back to the old ceremony of 'putting on of wreaths.'"

Maria smiles. "I still have the wreaths from my wedding. They've brought your father and me much happiness."

"Will you show them to me, Mom?"

"Perhaps later. We have a lot to do today."

Rada trails her fingers along the flowers on the finished crown. "Helena's crown is beautiful. Ouch!" She sucks on her finger. "Maybe you should have removed the thorns."

"They're supposed to keep her safe from misfortune. Even the wreath's circle shape has protective powers." Maria inserts the first rose into Simeon's crown. "And I left a piece of red thread, a coin, and a roll in the vineyard to make sure the vines retained their power."

Rada places Helena's wreath on her head and dances around the room. "Maybe I'll get married and have a traditional ceremony after all. This is going to be a fun day."

Baba chuckles and looks at Maria. They both shrug their shoulders.

When Niki comes out of his room, wearing jeans and a short-sleeve shirt, Maria gasps. "Niki! Change into your holiday outfit. This is a wedding, not a picnic."

He pouts as he shuffles next to his grandmother. "I don't want to change, and I don't want to go to a boring wedding."

"This is the time of year when a lot of people have weddings," Baba replies. "We all have to look our best because your mother and father are the *kum* and *kuma*. It's an honor. They're the next most important people at the wedding after the bride and groom."

"It's not an honor to me," Niki grumbles.

"Change, and I'll tell you a story about St. Demetrius so you'll understand his holiday today."

After a few minutes, Niki returns wearing black pants, a white shirt with red embroidery, a long, woolen cloak, and a fur cap decked with flowers and boxwood. He sits next to Baba.

"How handsome you look, but take off the *burnoose* and cap inside. You'll get too hot."

He slips them off. "You'll tell me a story now?"

Baba clears her throat. "A long time ago, St. Demetrius loaded three boats with grain he planned to sell. He set sail on the Danube River in the northern part of Bulgaria."

"Was he going to Germany? I learned in school the river starts there."

"I think he was going the other way, to the Black Sea, to sell wheat to the eastern countries."

"I also learned—"

Baba puts her finger to his lips. "Tell me later, please, so I can finish the story before we leave."

When he folds his hands and sits quietly, Baba continues. "A storm blew up suddenly, and the boat rocked back and forth. St. Demetrius feared they would sink, so he prayed. 'Lord, please calm the winds and save us. I want to build three monasteries with the money from the wheat. I promise I'll get married in the first one when it's built. In the second one, I'll pardon the sins of brave men and women, and in the third, I'll baptize children into your kingdom.' God accepted the saint's pledge and ordered the winds to stop their fury. St. Demetrius did as he'd promised when each church was built."

"People get married today because it's *Dimitrovden*?"

"Yes. Today is the end of the harvest. Wheat and water in the story are both symbols of life. It means we continue the cycle of life by getting married and having babies."

"Ugh. I don't want any babies," Niki snorts.

Maria pokes her head into the room. "Your father and Rada are ready to go. You can think about all the wonderful food at the wedding instead."

Georgi picks up the *uruglitsa*, the wedding banner, a red and white flag sewn onto a six-foot pole with red thread like that used for a *martenitsa*. Flowers, ivy, and strings of popcorn twist around the pole he cut from an apple tree a week ago. Red pins attach an apple wrapped in gold foil above the flag.

"Can I eat that apple?" Niki asks. "I'm starving."

"No, that's for the bride and groom after the wedding reception."

# Mary and Golden Apples

*In Christian lore, Mary once planted three trees that produced golden apples. She entrusted them to Michael to guard. These golden apples play a role in fertility rites in the church of the Dormition of Mary (The Golden Apple) in Gorni Voden in southern Bulgaria. People say the icon of Mary holding a golden apple produces miracles for women unable to bear children. One local story tells of a bed-ridden woman who was unable to go to church to pray to Mary for a child. She asked relatives to light candles for her and to give Mary an apple as a gift. Soon afterward, the woman recovered from her illness and became pregnant.*

*Childless women or married couples often make pilgrimages to the church and perform rituals to enable them to conceive. Mary's icon is decorated with apples and wreaths made of leaves from an apple tree. The priest first reads a prayer for childbirth, then the man and woman eat an apple, divided between them.* [25]

**First Snow**

Large snowflakes float to the ground as the family walks to the car. Maria says, "Snow today means it'll rain on *Gergiovden.*"

Niki sticks out his tongue to catch a snowflake. "St. Demetrius is shaking his beard. Do we get to roll in the snow afterwards?"

Rada catches a few in her hand. "We can after we change into our regular clothes, if enough of it sticks to the ground. Do you know why we do that?"

"Because it's fun?"

"Yeah, and rolling in the first snow makes us healthy. If you rub your face it in, you won't get headaches."

"If I rub *your* face in it, does that mean you won't get headaches?"

"Niki, behave today, please," Maria scolds.

Baba puts her arm around Niki and leads him to the car. "Did you know once, long ago, it didn't snow. It was warm all year long."

"No winter?"

"Maybe Baba will tell you the story before your father drops her off at church," Maria says.

"You're not coming with us now, Mom?" Niki asks.

"No, your father's bringing Baba to church and Rada to Helena's. The two of you are going to Simeon's, then coming back here for me." She kisses each of them good-bye, then returns to the house.

Baba gets into the back and Niki slides in next to her.

"It's true. Once there was no snow. Only lots of sunshine," Baba says. "Everything grew all year. People, animals, and plants increased in numbers. Some of the animals grew bold and considered themselves equal to people. One snake even tried to marry a human bride."

---

[25] Baeva, Vihra, "A Local Cult, a Universal Symbol: The Golden Apple in Gorni Voden, Southern Bulgaria," Our Europe, Ethnography – Ethnology – Anthropology of Culture, Vol. 2/2013, pp. 73-88, http://www.ptpn.poznan.pl/Wydawnictwo/czasopisma/our/OE-2013-073-088-Baeva.pdf.

"He must have wanted Rada." Niki snickers. "No one else does."

"Hey, you." Rada twists around from the front seat and scowls at her brother.

Baba reaches for Niki's hands. "The bride the snake wanted was a king's daughter. The snake thought he could become the next ruler. The king was so worried that other reptiles would begin demanding human brides that he prayed for the earth to become cold enough for snakes and frogs to freeze. The next day God sent a blizzard. Snow and ice covered everything."

"Was it *Baba Marta Den*? She likes to make it snow when she's angry."

"It could have been, Niki," Baba replies. "Ever since then, we've had both summer and winter."

## Did you know...?

Snow that appears to be black is an omen of epidemics, and snow that shines red in the sun's glow is a sign of war.

"Snow isn't always bad," Georgi comments.

"Thick snow, thick loaf of bread," Niki chants.

"That's right," Baba says. "Snow protects the soil. The land has to rest during the winter so it'll be strong in the spring and produce a lot of wheat."

Georgi says, "Snow is bad only if we've had droughts in summer and downpours in fall."

"Why?" Niki asks. "What does that mean?"

"The poor will be hungry, but the rich will prosper even more. Look," Georgi points out the window to cows grazing in the field.

"What? Just some cows."

"But see how they're licking themselves?"

Niki presses his face onto the glass. "Yah. So?"

"They're licking the front of their bodies. That means the first part of winter is going to be cold, then it'll get warmer."

"Does that mean if they licked their backsides, winter would be colder near the end?"

"Exactly." Georgi pulls into the church driveway and helps Baba out, then drives Rada to Helena's. "We'll see you later after we pick up the groom. I'll be leading them with the banner."

"Be ready to defend yourselves against the bridesmaids." Rada winks.

## The Worthy Groom

Simeon flings the door open as soon as Georgi knocks. "Good. You have the *uruglitsa*. You did manage to chop the branch off with one stroke, didn't you?"

"Yes, don't worry. It'll bring you luck."

"I want to add a hand-woven kerchief Helena made." His hands tremble as he wraps red thread around the pole, securing his future wife's gift.

When Simeon steps into a side room, Niki asks, "Why is he so worried about a stick and cloth?"

"It's a symbol of the Tree of Life, and the golden apple represents the sun. Both those and all the decorations are for health and fertility. They want to have lots of babies."

"Ugh, not babies again."

"Simeon!" someone yells. "It's time for us to shave your stubble and trim your hair."

"Yah," another person says, "you're no longer a boy, but a responsible man."

Other friends taunt him. "Let's tame that hair like Helena's going to tame you."

"No more wild days of youth."

The men sing ceremonial songs while they perform their tasks. When they're done, they dump bowls of wheat over Simeon's head. Then his brother goes outside and shoots a gun into the air. "That should frighten any spirits away," he says when he returns. "Let the wedding begin."

Simeon approaches his parents. "Bless me on this journey of life."

"Be fruitful and multiply as the Lord commands," they say.

The men leave the house and return to Georgi's to pick up Maria, the *kuma*. Simeon gives Georgi wine and choice cuts of meat, then everyone walks to Helena's house, dancing and singing. Georgi leads the group, waving the banner proudly. When Helena's house is in sight, a few bridesmaids jump out from behind bushes and rush forward, waving branches at the men.

"Why are they fighting?" Niki asks his father.

"They're only pretending to assault us. The groom is like a hero setting out on a noble quest. This is one of his adventures along the way. He has to fight off attackers and prove to his future bride he's strong and brave."

The women run back to the house laughing.

## The Respected Bride

Helena's friends sing as they braid her hair. When they're done, Rada says, "From girl to woman. No longer a wild *Samodiva* with hair flowing in the breeze. From now on, you'll bind your hair and keep your head covered with a scarf. We'll all show our respect to you."

"I'm really getting married." Helena blushes. "I can't wait to see Simeon."

"He was so nervous when we attacked him," a girl says. "He almost jumped a mile high."

"Is the *kumovo* tree done?" Helena asks Rada.

"Yes. It's from our apple tree." She gets it for Helena to inspect. "See, we decorated all five branches with flowers, vines, and a golden apple, just like the banner my dad made."

"It's lovely." Helena lays it next to her. "I have to hurry and get dressed. Simeon will be here soon."

Her friends hug her and help her put on the traditional wedding clothes. First her long white robe with red embroidery along the sleeves and neckline. Over that a dark brown *sukman*, the sleeveless dress her mother made, embroidered along the neckline and skirt hem. Finally, she puts a belt with golden decorations around her waist.

Helena pauses before she slips on a golden bracelet. "Simeon's father—"

"Your *svekur*," one of her friends giggles.

"Yes, my father-in-law, or soon to be one, gave me this last night."

Rada examines it. "It's lovely and seems quite expensive. I guess that means he likes you and has given his blessing for the wedding."

Music of *tupan* and *gaida* fill the air.

"They're here," a girl by the window squeals. "Quick. Look. They're trying to get in the gate."

"I can hear Niki now." Rada laughs. "He'll ask Dad, 'Why did they lock the gate? I thought Helena wanted to get married.' Then Dad'll say—"

"Wait," Helena says. "Your dad's turning toward Niki now." She opens the window and Georgi's words drift up: "It's part of Simeon's hero adventure to prove he can capture Helena's house and her heart, so he can take her home with him."

The girls laugh because Rada's prediction was accurate. Then they run downstairs to greet the wedding party. Helena's father opens the door to persistent knocking. Simeon paces outside.

Simeon's brother steps forward. "May I please have Helena's shoe?" When Helena's father holds it out, Simeon's brother places a golden coin in it. "Here's money for our entry."

Maria gives the wreaths for the wedding ceremony to Simeon's mother. Then she approaches Helena and hands her gifts of wine, candles, and candies. "You're a beautiful bride, but you need your veil."

"Okay," Helena says, but Rada nudges her.

"You have to refuse twice, then you can let my mom put it on you."

"I forgot." Helena backs away. "No, not yet. Please sit, everyone."

Maria steps closer. "The red veil will prevent adversity in your marriage. Let me put it on you now."

"Soon."

"It's so lovely," Maria persists. "Don't you want to wear it?"

Helena touches the fine silk cloth. "Yes, please."

Maria attaches the veil. Simeon then holds Helena's hand, and they go outside. Everyone sings a farewell song as the two of them drive away toward the church.

Georgi picks up the *kumova* tree, and he and the rest of the guests follow the bride and groom.

## The Wedding Celebration

When the Pavlovs drive over a bridge, Rada turns to Niki. "Do you remember the story of Enio and Stana from *Eniovden*?"

"Yah. The girl jumped into the river and drowned."

"It was a story about marriage, too. Water is symbolic of the bride passing from her home to a foreign land. Kind of like what our ancestors did when they came here."

"Helena's not going to jump in the river, is she?" Niki peers at the fast-flowing water. "I thought she wanted to get married."

"She's quite happy. I don't think we have to worry she'll try to drown herself."

The Pavlovs enter the church and sit with Baba, close to the altar. The air is filled with the scent of wax from candles lit beneath icons of saints lining the walls. The groom's parents stand next to the priest, holding the wreaths. Everyone waits for Simeon and Helena.

Baba whispers to Niki. "Watch their feet. They should both step over the threshold at the same time with their right feet first."

Niki looks closely as the bride and groom enter. "They did! What does that mean, Baba?"

"They'll be together forever."

The ceremony is short. The priest holds two lit candles while he prays to God to bless the couple. Simeon and Helena recite their vows and exchange rings. The priest crowns them with the wreaths, says a blessing, and reads passages in the Bible about marriage. Finally, husband and wife drink from a glass of wine. As they leave the church, everyone sprinkles them with corn, small coins, dried fruit, and sweets to make them fertile. Then all the guests return to Simeon's house to continue the celebration.

At the threshold. the couple steps on a white cloth strewn with flower petals. Inside, Simeon's mother welcomes the bride and groom. She breaks a couple chunks from a round *pitka* decorated with two doves, and hands each of them a piece.

Helena makes a face after she takes a bite. "That's salty."

"As salty as the difficulties you and Simeon will have in your married life," his mother says, then she hands them a second piece of bread, this one covered with honey. "Now eat this, too."

"Mmm. Much better."

"Marriage is also filled with much sweetness." She repeats the ritual with Maria and Georgi. "As *kum* and *kuma*, you must be with Simeon and Helena in both their good times and hard ones."

Families sit at tables scattered around the room. Maria places the *kumova* tree into a loaf of bread at their table.

Niki pokes the bread. "Mom, why's it decorated with snakes? It's not *Blagovets*."

"It represents the family's guardian snake. Simeon's mother probably left a bit of wine on a corner table for the snake, too, so he'll protect everyone, not just their family."

At the wedding table, Simeon and Helena pick up a round loaf of bread.

"Let's see who gets the bigger piece," Rada says.

The newly married couple pull on the bread until it breaks. Helena holds the larger chunk.

Rada laughs. "Poor Simeon. Helena's going to have the final say in the family. I knew she'd win. She's always been bossy."

## Birth of St. Demetrius and St. George

While the festivities proceed around them, a woman passes the Pavlov's table, pushing two infants in a stroller. "Twins," Rada gets up to look at them. "They're so cute. What're their names?"

"Dimitar and Georgi." The woman smiles, then covers the boys with a blanket before she leaves.

"Niki, did you know St. Dimitar had a twin named Georgi?" Baba asks him.

"Uh-huh." Niki slides his chair closer to Baba. "Will you tell me a story about them?"

"Yes." Baba sets her drink on the table. "Once a poor fisherman and his wife lived in a small village much like ours. They had no children, and even their horse wouldn't foal."

"No ponies? If they lived here, they could try to get one of the wild horses."

"They might be hard to catch," Baba says. "He didn't want a wild horse anyway. He was more interested in catching fish for their meal since all they'd had for a long time was berries from the forest."

Niki looks around at all the food. "And we have so much."

"We do. The man and his wife were grateful for what they did have. They were healthy, and they had each other. But they were lonely without children."

"Did they pray to God for some?"

"I'm sure they did." Baba shifts her position in the hard wooden chair. "He also praised God when he caught a small fish, even though it was barely enough for a meal. But then the fish spoke to him."

"Really?"

"Yes. The fish trembled and begged the man, 'Please toss me back into the sea.' The man felt pity for the tiny creature and let it go. He rowed home and searched for more berries for their meal."

Niki frowns. "I wish we could give him something."

"You're a good boy." Baba pats the top of his head. "A few weeks later, the man caught the same fish again. This time it was larger, enough to ease the ache of his hunger. Once again the fish asked him to spare its life, so the man set it back into the water, and it disappeared under the waves."

"Poor man." Niki sticks a fork into the fish on his plate.

"Yes, he was merciful. He went fishing again a few weeks later. He groaned when he caught the fish a third time. It was large enough for a meal for both him and his wife, but he was ready to let the fish go when it spoke. 'Don't release me this time. Cook me for yourself and your wife. Then bury my bones under your mare's manger.' The man hesitated, but he was so hungry he did what the fish ordered."

"I don't think I'd want to eat a talking fish."

Baba smiles. "It would be awkward. The fish was a magic one. Because the man did as the fish told him, his wife gave birth to Dimitar and Georgi. And the horse birthed two foals as well."

"A red one and a white one like the ones they ride?"

"Quite possibly."

113

**Final Rituals**

After the meal, while everyone dances. Simeon and Helena join the Pavlovs at their table.

Rada clasps Helena's hands. "I'm so happy for you, but how are you going to make it all the way through winter until *Todorovden* without speaking to your mother-in-law?"

Helena winks. "Maybe I'll be brave like you and start a new tradition."

"You? What's your plan?"

Helena leans forward and whispers, "I'll forbid my mother-in-law from doing any talking!"

The girls cover their mouths and giggle at the prospect.

Georgi clears his throat, and they turn toward him as he takes apart the banner. He gives the cloth to Helena, then he breaks the pole. "The same way this pole is broken, you must break from your family, Helena, and start a new branch with your husband. This ensures the Tree of Life goes on forever."

He removes the apple, unwraps the golden foil, and hands it to Helena. "Both of you, take a bite from this now. Apples are a sign of health and fertility." Finally, Georgi hands Helena the *kumova* tree. "Keep this in your husband's home. This symbolizes that the two of you are now a family."

# Arkhangelovden

**St. Michael**

*Arkhangelovden* is a celebration for Archangel Michael, or Rangel, often called "the angel of death." When people pass from this life into the next one, Orthodox Christians believe he drags their souls out of their bodies with his sword. A popular saying is, if a person dies smiling, St. Michael has given him a golden apple in exchange for his soul. The archangel, along with St. Peter, weighs souls of both rich and poor on a set of scales to see if the deceased are worthy to enter heaven.

As part of the celebration, on the Saturday before *Arkhangelovden*, families gather at cemeteries, or at

# All Souls' Days

*Bulgarians celebrate several All Souls' Days throughout the year.*

- *The first,* Golyama, ***Great***, *occurs in the spring, a week before Easter Lent. This is a time when Christians prepare to share in the suffering and resurrection of Christ.*
- Spassovden, ***Ascension*** *day, takes place forty days after Easter. The belief is that the door to the afterlife opens on Maudy Thursday, the first Great Thursday, and closes on* Spassovden, *which is also called the last Great Thursday. People pray that wandering souls will return to the spirit world.*
- *The next,* Chereshova, ***Cherry***, *happens in the summer, on the Saturday before Pentecost. It gets its name from fruit trees that blossom during this season.*
- Arkhangelova, ***Souls***, *or* Golyama Zadoushnitsa, *takes place in the fall, right before Arkhangelovden. This is the final and greatest All Souls' Day of the year. It's a time for the living to beg forgiveness for their deceased loved ones.*

a friend's house, to hold a memorial for departed loved ones. They bring a ritual meal consisting of a round loaf of bread, boiled wheat with walnuts and honey, and wine. Each item is symbolic. *Rangelovo blyudo*, or "Rangel's meal," the ritual bread dedicated to the saint, is made with images of the cross in remembrance of the dead. This is similar to bread prepared for burial ceremonies in which relatives leave a loaf for the deceased to take with him on his journey to the afterlife. People call the bread "kind soul." It's always broken, never cut, so its soul isn't hurt. Grains of wheat represent the soul's immortality, because when planted, wheat dies and a new life grows from the seed. Wine is the symbol of blood and life, and indicates the transition between life and death.

## ~ ORIGINS ~

The cycle of life—birth, death, and rebirth in a new form—is seen everywhere in nature. The same is true in human life. Although people debate what the soul is, those who have confidence it exists say it lives on after the body dies.

The ancient Thracians also believed in the immortality of the soul. Death was not something to fear. A ruler's wives often competed to have him choose her as his "favorite." When he died, the winner had the honor of being ritually slain, allowing her to continue into the next life with her husband. Ancient writers like Herodotus also described the Thracians as people who mourned births but rejoiced at burials, because they believed the dead were alive in perfect happiness in another realm.

### Did you know...?

In Bulgaria, people publish obituaries not only in newspapers, but families also place them at bus stops, on telephones posts, and other locations. Some people mistakenly think these flyers are missing person's posters. Relatives perform this custom after the person dies, again in forty days, and once more after six months.

Another popular belief was that the soul was connected to a person's shadow and his breath. Without both, he would die. The soul went in and out of a human's body through his breath. It was once the custom to trap someone's shadow in a wall, bridge, or fountain to make the structure strong. But then, once the person's shadow separated from his body, he would become ill and die, and his breath, and soul, would leave his body as well. The shadow then haunted and protected the place as a *talasuhm* in the form of a dog, cat, or other animal.

### Soul's Journey

As Christianity took hold in Bulgaria, beliefs about the soul changed. When a person was born, God not only gave him a soul, but also an angel, *hranitel*, to guide and protect him from misfortune. However, Satan, or Dennitza, the fallen angel sent a devil, *pakostnik* or rascal, to harm the person and condemn his soul. Throughout the person's life, these two beings fought for control. At the person's death, his soul did not immediately go to heaven or damnation. The angel and devil took him on a forty-day journey to all the places he'd been in life. At the end of the travels, a righteous person was offered the choice to return to his life or continue to heaven. People believed that once the soul glimpsed the freedom and beauty eternity had to offer, none desired to return to his former life. Instead, the soul began its final journey to the afterlife.

To prepare a person's soul for the first stage of this journey—walking across a barren field immersed in darkness—his relatives lit candles so he could find the right path. Next the soul had to pass over a field covered with weeds and thorns. For this, his kin left him a pair of shoes. The final hurdle for the soul to overcome was crossing a fiery river. To pay the boatman, the soul used coins people left in his hands or the ones thrown into the grave. The soul had to hang onto a flax fiber or hair strung above the river. If he was righteous, he could cross in safety. If he deserved damnation, he fell into an abyss.

**Golden Apples**

Apples have been a symbol of death and immortality since before Adam and Eve ate the forbidden fruit in the garden of Eden. Although the Bible doesn't say the fruit was an apple, it has often been described this way in art and literature.

The apple's spherical shape has been equated with eternity. In addition, the core forms a pentacle, five-pointed star, a symbol associated with magic and pagan rites performed for the Mother Goddess. The fruit is also an ancient symbol of health and fertility, since the pentacle signifies life and well-being.

## ~ RITUALS IN PRACTICE ~

On the Saturday before *Arkhangelovden*, the Pavlovs gather at the gravesite of Dayado Georgi, Grandfather Georgi, after the church memorial service. Baba kneels by the gravestone and places flowers on the ground. Niki comes over, sits by her, and holds her hand.

"When Saint Michael came so many years ago, I hoped he'd sit at my Georgi's feet, so he'd recover." Baba's voice cracks, and she looks at Niki. "But God wanted your grandfather, so the Archangel chose to sit by his head instead. Your dayado smiled right before he left, so I knew Michael gave him a shiny golden apple in exchange for his soul."

"I don't like St. Michael for taking Dayado. I can't remember him."

"You were a baby at the time. Dayado was so proud of you." Baba strokes Niki's hair. "St. Michael doesn't want to be cruel. My Georgi was ill. It was a blessing St. Michael took him quickly so he didn't suffer. Let me tell you a story about the saint and golden apples."

**Golden Apple Tree**

"A long time ago, a little girl was seriously ill—"

"How old was she? My age? What did she have?"

"I think she was three of four. No one knew what was wrong with her. She weakened and became paler every day until all she could do was stay in bed." Baba folds her hands in her lap. "The innocent child was righteous in God's eyes, and the saint wanted to take her to heaven so she wouldn't suffer. For several days, he tried to reach the girl, but her moans and the anguished cries of her parents drove him away. Night after night, the parents never left the girl's side."

"What's St. Michael going to do?"

"God thought about it, then came up with a plan. He planted an apple tree in the yard outside the girl's window. The tree grew overnight, and three golden apples appeared on its branches."

"Golden? Like the ones we wrapped foil around for Helena's wedding?"

"No, Baba says. "The skin on these was golden, not red. They were beautiful. St. Michael returned to the house. He gave one apple to the mother and another to the father. He told them to give the final one to the little girl.""

"Did they eat them? I wonder if they tasted funny."

"I don't think they ate them. They were a special gift," Baba says. "When the mother handed the apple to her daughter, the little girl smiled and her cheeks turned rosy. The girl's parents thought she was recovering, so they went outside to look at the marvelous tree the apples came from."

"Did any more apples grow on it?"

"No, only those three. Since the parents now had hope that their daughter would get better, their grief didn't block the saint from the girl's bedroom. While they were outside, he approached her. She thanked him for the apple and said she was ready to go with him. He reached out with his sword and helped her soul leave her body."

Niki clenches his fist. "She died? I bet her parents were mad at the saint for tricking them."

"They were heartbroken, but in time they realized their daughter wasn't in any more pain, and they were happy the saint took her to heaven." Baba sighs. "After that, St. Michael asked God to be merciful and make him deaf so he could collect souls without having to hear all that pain time after time."

"He's deaf? How can he hear our prayers?"

"He hears them in his heart, where compassion for the dying dulls the pain."

## Did you know...?

*The righteous often die an easy death on major feast days, while wicked people die painful deaths, their souls fighting against leaving the body, knowing the suffering they will endure for eternity.* [26]

## Honoring the Dead

Maria, Georgi, and Rada join Niki and Baba. Georgi holds out his hand to help his mother up. "We're ready to begin the ceremony." He hands Baba a lit candle. "Let's remember my father."

Baba stoops and places the votive candle onto her husband's grave. "A candle to light your presence, so our memories of you don't die."

Georgi gives her a *baklitsa*. She pours wine from it in three circles to the left of the marble cross, the first where her husband's head lies, the next halfway down, and the final one at his feet. After handing the *baklitsa* back to her son, Baba makes the sign of the cross three times. She reaches into a basket, breaks a piece from some bread, and lays it onto the grave. Then she looks through the basket again, removes a piece of baklava and boiled wheat, mixed with walnuts, honey, and cookie crumbs. While she places them next to the bread, she says, "God grant peace to my beloved husband's soul. Let this food nourish him in the other world."

Georgi says, "Peace to Daydo's soul. May St. Michael deliver us from iniquity and grant us a peaceful death."

Maria lights incense, and its smoke drifts around the cross.

Baba turns to Niki and whispers, "Did you know Satan fears incense?"

"He does? I didn't think he was afraid of anything."

"Incense cleanses wickedness, so it keeps him away."

---

[26] Note: This is an old, popular saying. It's not suggesting that everyone who dies a painful death is wicked.

Niki glances around. "I'm glad. I don't want to see him."

The ceremony completed, Maria picks up the basket.

Niki pokes around in it. "I'm hungry. Can I have some?"

"We'll eat later at home. This is to share." She walks around the cemetery, greeting other families and giving them food.

Peter leaves the grave of his brother Pavel. He hands Maria food he brought, saying "God forgive."

She repeats, "God forgive," then gives him some of what she brought.

"Mom, why do you say that?" Niki asks,

"Our guardian angels protect us with their prayers, so we ask forgiveness for our deceased relatives."

## Shadow and Breath

While Maria continues to greet other families, Baba relaxes on a bench, and Rada and Niki sit with her. Baba stretches out her legs. "Let me tell you a story. In 1469, three brothers were building the Kadin Bridge in the southeast. Every time they made progress, they returned the next day to discover the raging waters had destroyed everything, and they had to start over. The eldest said, 'The only way we can make the foundation strong enough is to build someone's shadow into it.'

"They argued about who should sacrifice his life to make the bridge strong. 'All of us are needed to work on the bridge,' the youngest said.

" 'Then it'll have to be one of our wives,' the middle brother decided. 'We'll trap the shadow of the first one who comes to the site tomorrow.'

"The youngest didn't like the idea, but both his brothers convinced him it was the only way. He went away fearing the worst. The two older brothers remained at the site and made plans to discourage their wives from coming the next day, saying they were taking a break from work. At noon the next day, the wife of the youngest brought her husband his meal. Heartbroken, he looked at his brothers, who only shrugged. 'It has to be done,' the eldest said.

" 'Struma,' the man said to his wife, 'I've dropped my wedding ring into the crevice in the wall. Will you find it for me?'

"When she stooped to look, the two older brothers hurried to build a wall around her shadow.

" 'Husband, what have you done?' She backed away from the brothers. 'What will happen to our child with me gone?'

"The youngest brother wept. Soon afterwards, his wife became ill and died. The brothers completed the bridge, and it still stands today against the strong waters of the river that now bears the name of the wife, Struma."

As Baba finishes the story, a butterfly lands on her hand. "My Georgi, you're here," she whispers, and tears fill her eyes.

# Nikulden

**December 6 – Никулден – Nikulden: St. Nicholas' Day.**
*Festival in honor of St. Nicholas, the Wonderworker, the saint associated with Christmas. He's the patron of children, fishermen, sailors, bankers, and merchants. He's also considered to be in charge of controlling all water bodies and reigns over creatures living in them. Often described as "Lord of the Sea," Nicholas is compared to the Greek god Poseidon. Born 280 A.D. Died Dec. 6, 343 A.D.*

St. Nicholas

*Nikulden*, in reverence to St. Nicholas, or Nikolas, is a favorite saint's feast day. He has various names in different parts of the world. Whether you know him as Father Christmas, St. Nick, or Santa Claus, his reputation for giving gifts makes him popular. Children leave stockings for him to fill on Christmas Eve. In Bulgaria, as well as in German-speaking countries, on the eve of December 5, children place wooden shoes by the fireplace, hoping the saint fills them with sweets, gifts, and coins.

The most famous story about the saint's generosity tells how he secretly threw three purses of gold coins through the window of a poor man's house for his three unmarried daughters. In those days, women needed a dowry to marry. Without marriage, a woman's life was even more harsh.

In some parts of Bulgaria, unmarried women leave gifts at the saint's icon in the church as part of pre-marriage rituals. Another custom is that those who have lost someone to the sea make wreaths, and toss them into the water in the departed's memory.

## Did you know...?

*A legend about cape Kaliakra in southern Bulgaria claims it was formed when St. Nicholas fled from Turkish soldiers. The earth extended into the sea to help him escape.*

Associated with these saint festivals comes the concept of name days, which is sometimes called a "half birthday." The festivity is like a birthday, but more popular. Instead of celebrating the day of a person's birth, people celebrate a day associated with that person's name. Most often, these are held on saint feast days. So, a person named Nicholas would celebrate his name day on December 6.

Those celebrating name days most often provide food and beverages for guests. Since everyone knows when it's another person's name day, no special invitations are needed. Anyone can drop by to wish the person a blessing and happiness on his special day. Visitors bring a small gift; in olden days, a common gift was a shirt, a bottle of wine, or an apron.

At one time, if people didn't want visitors on their name day, they placed ads in the paper stating they wouldn't be receiving guests.

## ~ ORIGINS ~

Long ago, a person's name was like a magic word, an amulet, or a spell. Knowing someone's name gave you power over him. Many fantasy novels work this fact into their storylines.

Even today, Bulgarians consider a person's name important. One proverb says, "The name makes the man," while another states, "A man with no name is no man." On a person's name day, it is customary to greet him with "Long live you and your name."

Name days may have come about because people in ancient times didn't know the exact date of their birth. They'd mention the day of their birth as "born after St. Demetrius' Day," "at threshing time," "before grape-picking," or "on Holy Virgin's Day."

People often named their children after saints, believing the saint would protect and bless the child. Over time, people associated the celebration of the saint's feast day more with their name than with the saint.

## ~ RITUALS IN PRACTICE ~

Outside the Pavlov house a snowstorm hisses in the gray sky. Inside, Balkan lies curled by the fireplace where a log burns and shoots sparks up the flue. Baba bustles around the kitchen, preparing traditional dishes for *Nikulden*, a day to honor St. Nicholas, and also Niki's name day. She rolls dough into small balls, flattens them into circles, and fries them in oil.

"Good morning," Rada says as she comes into the room. "I'm starving. Something smells delicious."

"It's *mekitsi*." Baba puts a plate of the fried dough made with yogurt, along with a jar of honey, onto the table. "It's one of Niki's favorites."

Rada pulls out a chair, but Niki flies into the room and plops down in her spot. "Hey, I was going to sit there!"

Niki sticks his tongue out, but doesn't move. Rada glares at him, then sits in another chair.

Baba wipes dough from her hands onto her apron. She reaches to ruffle Niki's hair.

He pulls back. "Your fingers are sticky."

She bends to kiss his cheek. "Happy name day, Nikolay. May you and your name be healthy, and may you continue to make us happy and proud."

"Yeah! It's *Nikulden*! Are we going to have guests?"

"Yes. You're old enough to have a proper celebration. Your parents invited friends to lunch after church service."

Rada and Niki both reach for the plate of *mekitsi* at the same time. "You go first," Rada says and pulls her hand back. "It's your special day after all. I got all the attention on *Arkhangelovden*. And I'm more special since I share my day with an *angel*, and not just a saint."

"Yah, the angel of *death*. I share it with St. Nicholas, the Wonderworker. He brings people to life instead of taking their souls." Niki stacks his plate high with fried dough.

"That's right, Niki." Maria comes into the room. "I think Baba's told you stories about St. Nickolas' miracles."

"Will you tell me another one, Baba?"

"How about the one where a carp obeyed him?" Baba asks. "That would be a good one since St. Nicholas is master of the sea and everything in it."

"Including *Rusalki*, the mermaids?" Niki asks.

"Yes, he rules them, and their sisters the *Samodivi*," Maria adds.

121

Baba moves two pans of bread to the back of the counter to rise. "First I have to finish making the dough for the *rybnik* for lunch."

"Mmmm. I love carp." Niki breaks off a small piece of *mekitsi* and holds it out for Balkan to gobble. The dog rubs his nose against Niki's leg and thumps his tail against the floor.

## Did you know...?

*Like bread and wine, fish are symbolic. They represent women's fertility, water's life-giving properties, the depths of the earth, or the underworld, where new life begins, and granting wishes. In Christianity, disciples were called fishers of men.*

"I like the crust the best," Rada tells Baba. "You should write down your recipes for Mom. You have so many secret ingredients."

"I think your mother's making improvements to my recipes." Baba winks. "She has her own secrets."

"I'm still learning from the master." Maria laughs, then turns to Baba. "Let me finish this so you can rest. Maybe tell Niki and Rada your story while we wait for Georgi to return with the carp." She pulls out rice, raisins, and walnuts from the pantry to make the stuffing.

"Mom, did Dad go fishing with Peter in this storm?" Rada peers out the window. Snow blows across the yard.

"No. He went into town to get a carp from the market. If there wasn't a storm, they would have fished from shore today, instead of going out in Peter's boat, as a sign of respect to St. Nicholas."

"And to honor the saint, they'd also eat the first fish they caught while they're still on shore," Baba adds.

### St. Nicholas and the Sinking Ship

Baba settles on the couch, and Niki and Rada sit on each side of her. "Besides being our patron saint and family protector, St. Nicholas was a miracle worker. One story tells about him travelling to the Holy Land to visit Christ's tomb. A mighty storm arose on the sea."

"Our sea? The Black Sea?" Niki asks.

"No," Baba says. "I think it was the Mediterranean Sea, since the Holy Land is in Israel."

"Oh. We get some bad storms here, too."

"We do," Baba replies. "This particular storm was quite fearsome. Lightning struck a sailor, killing him instantly."

Niki raises a fisted hand and brings it down quickly. "Ka-boom!"

"Just like that." Baba smiles. "Terrified people ran around, not knowing what to do. Another sailor shouted, 'The storm damaged the ship! We have to stop the water from pouring in, or we'll all drown!' "

"Is this where St. Nicholas performs his miracle?" Niki asks.

"First, he prayed," Baba says. " 'Lord, save your people. Show them your mighty power.' When he finished speaking, a huge silver carp jumped into the hole, stopping the water from coming into the boat."

"That's why people say the carp is St. Nicholas' servant," Rada adds.

"Very true," Baba says. "The saint also performed another miracle. He placed his hands on the dead sailor and again raised his voice to God. 'Lord, return your servant to this world so he may continue to support his family.' The man immediately sat up. He looked around, stunned. The storm had quieted and people were cleaning up the damage."

Rada stands and straightens her dress. "That's why we revere him as patron of sailors and fishermen."

"When he's angry, he can also send storms and hurricanes to punish people," Baba says.

Niki gets up and looks out the window. "I wonder who he's angry at today. The wind's blowing snow all over."

"Our feast in his honor should appease him. We'll pray to him to help and protect us, and also ask him to pray to the Lord for our forgiveness," Baba says.

## Silver Carp and Ritual Meal

"Dad's home!" Niki rushes to open the door. A cold blast of air rattles pictures on the wall. "Dad! Did you know today's my name day? Baba says I'm grown up now so I can have visitors."

Georgi stomps snow from his boots. "Happy name day. God bless your name and our house." He looks toward Maria and winks, then hands Niki the large bag he's holding. "A grownup, huh? Here, then. You can give this to your mother."

Niki grasps the bag and drags it while shuffling to the kitchen. With a grunt, he lifts it onto the chair, climbs next to it, and heaves it onto the table. Finally, he rips open the bag. "Wow! This is the biggest fish I've ever seen! Mom, Baba, Rada, look at it! It's a magical carp with silver scales that look like coins."

Balkan scampers over and lifts his nose, sniffing.

"Thanks, Dad." Niki wraps his arm around his father and snuggles into Georgi's shoulder.

Maria puts the carp into a large, shallow dish. "I want everyone to help so we can get done quicker and be ready to go to church at noon. Baba can get the table ready. Niki, go with your father to get more wood for the fireplace. Rada will make *sarmi* and stuffed peppers, and I'll finish the *rybnik* and make beans and corn."

"No meat in the *sarmi*, right, Mom?" Rada takes grape leaves and vegetables from the refrigerator.

"Yes, not during Christmas Lent. Only vegetarian dishes, except for the fish."

Rada gets a *guvetch* from the cupboard and sets the colorful clay pot aside to put the stuffed grape leaves in when she's finished. She chops vegetables and fries them in a pan along with rice, and Baba's mix of spices.

Maria cleans the carp, removes its scales and bones, and sets aside the cross-shaped bone from its head. "Next time I'll show you how to clean it properly, Rada. You have to be careful not to let the scales fall. If anyone steps on them, they'll get sick and die." She finishes washing the carp, coats it with strips of dough representing the fish's spine, tail and eyes, and places it and the bread into the oven.

## Did you know...?

*Cleaning the scales off a fish makes it "naked." This is symbolic of poverty and represents St. Nicholas, who gave up his wealth to help the poor.*

Niki and Georgi dump wood onto the hearth. After Niki shakes snow out of his hair, he wanders to the kitchen. He pokes the bones and scales, then picks up the one Maria set aside. "What's this for?"

"That's something I'm going to sew into your cap," Baba says. "It'll ward off disease and *uroki*, bad spirits."

"Are you going to do that with the rest of the bones, too?"

"No. Those are sacred. They should be buried or burned to make sure our family stays healthy and the land is fertile in the spring."

"Like how we bury lamb bones on *Gergiovden*?" Rada asks.

"Yes. After the storm passes, I'll place these in the sea." Baba takes a towel from a drawer and gently places the bones into it.

Niki holds out his hand. "I'll help you, Baba. I'm grown up now. I can send them out to sea."

She smiles and gives them to him. "Place them out of the way for now."

Soon the bread and carp are done. Mouth-watering aromas drift from their golden crusts as Maria removes them from the oven.

Georgi says, "The other women will have a hard time making theirs look better than yours. They may even be jealous when you present the bread and carp for the priest to bless."

### Church Service

At the church, incense and candle wax mix with the aroma of freshly baked bread. Rada shivers and shuffles her feet under the pew. She sits closer to Baba, but chills run down her spine. "Why did I wear heels?" she mutters to herself. "I'm not so elegant with goose bumps."

The beating of wings breaks the monotony of the Holy Father's deep, low voice. Rada looks up toward the dome, painted with Biblical scenes, as a dove flies toward the rudder-shaped window, trying to get in.

At the end of the service, the priest blesses the bread and carps everyone brought. Baba hands him a loaf of ritual bread wrapped in a white cloth. "Happy *Nikulden*. May Nicholas keep your family and relatives healthy and safe."

Maria and her family then chat with other villagers. She spots Peter and waves him over. "Have a piece of bread, and make sure you come to celebrate Niki's name day."

"I'll try to make it." Peter pats Niki on the head. "Happy name day. May your name be alive and healthy."

Maria sighs as he walks away. "Since Pavel was lost at sea, Peter's changed so much. I keep encouraging him to get out and visit people."

"He'll come around when he's ready. Don't worry," Georgi says. "We should get home now. Guests will be arriving soon."

### Niki's Celebration

Maria places food onto the table. The *rybnik* resembles the ritual loaves of bread, which are decorated like a carp. Someone knocks at the door, and Georgi greets the first guests. After a few more arrive, he begins the ceremony by raising the bread over his head and breaking it in half.

Relatives and friends arrive throughout the day. Each brings a small gift, some for Niki's name day, others for the family. Chocolate, fruit, and wine collect on the counter. Children's laughter, cheers, and clapping come from Niki's room, where he opens gifts. The table remains set the entire day, open to anyone who chooses to visit.

Finally, the last person leaves. Rada helps her mother clean the kitchen. "Should I leave food to welcome our ancestral spirits in case they stop by tonight?"

"Yes, leave a little bread and a glass of wine."

After everyone says good night, it takes a long time for Niki to fall asleep. He's still excited about his first name day with guests. The thumping of Balkan's tail by Niki's bedside eventually lulls the boy to sleep, and he dreams of riding a tall, swift ship. All along the side, silver carp frolic in the blue sea.

# Selected Saint Name Days

| Day | Saint | Holiday | A Few Names of Those Who Celebrate |
|---|---|---|---|
| Jan 1 | St. Vasilius or Basil | Survaki and Vasilyovden | Vasil(ka), Vasko/a, Veselin(a), Vessie |
| Jan 2 | St. Sylvester | Sylvestrovden | Sylvia, Sylvester, Goran, Goritsa |
| Jan 7 | St. John the Baptist | Ivanovden | Ivan(ka), Enio, Ivet, Yoan/na, Jan, Jean, Iva |
| Jan 17 | St. Anthony | Antonovden | Anton(ia), Donna, Donny, Tonyo, Tony |
| Jan 18 | St. Athanasius | Atanasovden | Atanas(ka), Nasso, Tanyu, Tinka |
| Feb 1 | St. Trifon | Trifonovden | Trifon, Trifonka, Lozan |
| Feb 10 | St. Haralambos | Charalambos | Hari, Harry, Valentin(a), Valery, Valeria |
| Feb 14 | St. Valentine | Trifonovden and Valentine's Day | Valentin, Valentina, Valyo/a |
| *Varies | St. Theodore | Todorovden | Todor(ka), Teodor(a), Theo, Dora, Toto |
| *Varies | St. Lazarus | Lazarovden | Lazar, Lazo, Lazarina, Lara, Lacho |
| May 6 | St. George | Gergiovden | Georgi, Gergana, Gina, Galina, Gosho, Joro |
| May 11 | St. Cyril/St. Methodius | Kiril i Metodi | Kiril(a), Metodi, Kiro, Kirilka, Metodiy(a) |
| May 21 | St. Constantine/Helena | Kostadinovden | Konstantin, Kostadin(ka), Elena, Eli, Elitsa |
| Jun 11 | St. Bartholomew | Vartolomey | Vartolomei |
| Jun 25 | St. Enio | Eniovden | Yanko, Yana, Yanka |
| Jun 29 | St. Peter | Petrovden | Peter, Kamen, Petrana, Apostol, Krum |
| Jun 30 | St. Paul | Pavlyovden | Pavel, Pavlina, Polya, Polina |
| Jul 8 | St. Procopius | Prokopi Pchelar | Prokopi |
| Jul 25 | St. Anna | Dormition of the Mother of the Holy Virgin | Anna, Yana, Enko, Ana, Anica, |
| Sep 1 | St. Simeon | Simeonovden | Simeon(a), Mona, Moncho |
| Oct 14 | St. Petka | Petkovden | Petko/a, Petyo, Petkana, Penka, Pencho |
| Oct 26 | St. Demetrius | Dimitrovden | Dimitar, Dimitrina, Mitra, Dragan, Drago |
| Nov 8 | St. Michael (Archangel) | Arkhangelovden | Angel(ina), Mihaill, Rada, Emil(ia), Rangel |
| Nov 30 | St. Andrew | Andreevden | Andrei, Andrey, Andriana |
| Dec 5 | St. Sava | Savinden | Sava, Slavka, Slav, Vladislav, Slavi, Sabi |
| Dec 6 | St. Nicholas | Nikulden | Nikola, Nikolay, Kolyo, Nikolina, Nina, Niko |
| Dec 9 | St. Anna | Aninden | Anna, Ana, Anita, Aneta, Anette, Anelia |
| Dec 12 | St. Spyridon | Spyridonovden | Spyridon, Spiro, Darina |
| Dec 20 | St. Ignatius | Ignazhden | Ignat, Ognyan(a), Plamen(a) |
| Dec 27 | St. Stephen | Stefanovden | Stefan(ka), Stanka, Tanyo/a, Stamen, Sonya |

*Varies with Easter.

# Name Days on Certain Other Holidays

| Day | Holiday | A Few Names of Those Who Celebrate |
|-----|---------|-----------------------------------|
| Jan 6 | Yordanovden or Bogoyavlenie (Epiphany) Christ's baptism in the Jordan river | Iordan(ka), Yordan, Dancho, Dana, Boyan |
| Jan 20 | Petlyovden (Rooster's Day) Health of small boys | Efthimios, Evtim, Euthim, Eftim, Efimir, Momchil |
| Mar 1 | Baba Marta Den Make *martenitsi* | Evdokiya, Marta, Martin, Martina, Boiko, Boyko |
| Mar 25 | Blagovets (Annunciation) Spring arrives | Blago/a, Bonka, Marian(a), Evangelina, Vangel, Dobri, Dobrina, Dobrinka |
| *Varies | Tsvetnitsa (Flower Day) or Vrubnitsa (Palm Sunday) Jesus rode into Jerusalem and proclaimed king | Tsvetelina, Lilia, Yavor, Yassen, Roza, Iglika, Violeta, Varban, Latinka, Temenuga, Karamfila, Zdravko, Kamelia |
| *Varies | Velikden, Easter Resurrection of Jesus | Anastas, Velichko/a, Veliko/a, Velko, Svetla, Svetozar |
| May 24 | Day of the Alphabet In honor of Saints Cyril and Methodius, who created the Cyrillic alphabet | Kiril(a), Metodi, Kiro, Kirilka, Metodiy(a) |
| *Varies | Spasovden Jesus ascended to Heaven | Spas, Spaska, Sotir, Spasena, Spasuna |
| *Varies | Pentecost or Holy Trinity The day the disciples received the Holy Spirit | Trayko, Trayan, Trayana |
| Aug 15 | Sveta Bogoroditsa (Holy Virgin) or Goliama Boboroditsa (Great Mary) The Assumption of Mary | Mara, Marian, Mariana, Maria, Mariyan, Masha, Mika, Mira, Mario, Marcho, Despina, Panaiot |
| Aug 29 | Seknovenie or Black Saint John The day John the Baptist was beheaded | Anastas, Anastasi, Anastasiya |
| Sep 8 | Rozhdestvo na Presveta Bogoroditsa (Virgin Mary's Nativity) or Small Mary | Ognyan, Ognyana |
| Sep 14 | Krustovden (The Holy Cross Day) Preparation for the grape harvest | Krustina, Krustyo, Krustan, Kancho, Stavri, Krastan, Krastina, Krastyo, Krastyu, Krastena |
| Sep 17 | Vyara, Nadezhda, Lyubov, Sophia (Faith, Hope, Love, and Sofia) Sofia and her daughters were martyred | Vyara, Vera, Veronika, Nadezhda, Nadya, Lyuben, Lyubomir, Lyuba, Sophia, Sofka, Sevda |
| Oct 1 | Pokrov Bogorodichen (Holy Protection of Mother of God) | Anani, Anania |
| Dec 24 | Budni Vecher (Christmas Eve) | Blagorodna, Evgeni, Evgenia, Zheni, Zhechka, Parvan, Parvana, Bistra, Bisser(a) |
| Dec 25 | Koleda (Christmas) | Hristo, Hristina, Kristian(a), Christina, Emil, Kolio, Bojin, Radostin, Radomir, Mladen |

*Varies with Easter.

# FALL: What Have You Learned?

1. Which rituals are performed for a Bulgarian wedding?
    A. Wearing wreaths of flowers or golden crowns.
    B. Attaching an apple covered with gold foil to the top of a pole.
    C. Eating a piece of salty bread and another covered with honey.
    D. All of the above.

2. Which statement below is true about saints?
    A. St. Demetrius shakes snow from his beard.
    B. St. George is famous for killing a dragon.
    C. St. Nicholas gave away all his money to help the poor.
    D. All are legends told about the saints.

3. Who is called "the angel of death"?
    A. Dionysus.
    B. *Samodivi*.
    C. St. Michael.
    D. The Grinch.

4. What creature is connected to St. Nicholas?
    A. Carp.
    B. Snake.
    C. Cuckoo.
    D. None of the above.

Answers: 1-D; 2-D; 3-C; 4-A.

# MARIA'S KITCHEN

*Traditional Bulgarian Food*

# Bulgarian Cuisine

Bulgaria's varied and colorful cuisine has been greatly impacted by ancient history, diverse traditions, and customs, as well as being influenced by the exquisite spiciness of the East and the elegance of European cooking. If you wonder why these dishes have a unique, unforgettable taste, it's due to the method in which food is cooked and the type of cookware used. In some regions, people still use "ancient" cooking equipment like embers and earthen ovens (*podnitza*). More commonly, though, they use colorful clay pots (*guvetch*) and copper or earthenware frying pans (*sach*). Food cooked in a clay pot doesn't require using unhealthy fat and needs only a small amount of liquid, so the food retains its nutrients and vitamins. Meats in particular remain tender.

Among the traditional Bulgarian dishes are beans cooked in a clay pot, meatless *sarmi* wrapped in grape or cabbage leaves, and stuffed dried peppers with rice or crushed beans. But the queen of all dishes is *banitsa* (cheese pie). Made everywhere in Bulgaria, it's prepared differently in each region, which contributes to its specific taste.

Another national specialty is *katmi*, similar to pancakes or crêpes, but a little thicker than the latter. The main ingredients vary, and may include milk, yogurt, eggs, yeast, and tap or sparkling water. It's best to cook them on a *sach* over an open fire, so the wood contributes to their unique flavor.

The variety and combination of spices used on the food also make the taste unforgettable. Some of the main ones are dill, mint, savory, and parsley. One of my favorite spices is *sharena sol*; its ingredients are summer savory, paprika, and sea salt. You can find this spice at the table of almost every Bulgarian home. Magical spices add not only to the taste, but to the aroma as they cook.

Bulgarian yogurt, which comes in more than one hundred varieties, is another important ingredient in many traditional Bulgarian foods. What could be better on a hot summer day than *tarator*? This cold soup, made from yogurt, water, finely grated cucumbers, garlic, and dill, is not only refreshing, but also healthy.

Don't forget a good wine to bring out the real taste of your gourmet meal. Similar to the different traditions and rituals, each region in Bulgaria has its own local wines. It's no wonder, since Bulgarians have been producing wine since the time of the Thracians. Wine lovers have a plethora of quality wines to choose from.

Or perhaps you prefer *rakiya*, a brandy made from plums or grapes with your meal. Or even *gyul*, rose brandy.

Whatever your choice, *Nazdrave*, "Cheers, to your health!" I hope you enjoy the traditional recipes that follow. As a bonus, I've added a modern twist to some to help you discover the diversity of the Bulgarian kitchen.

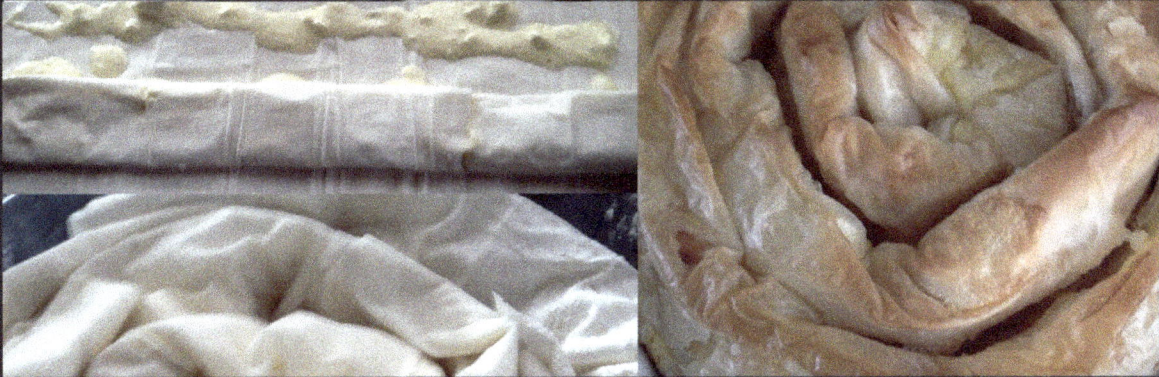

# Banitsa

1 lb (500 g) feta cheese
1 1/2 cups yogurt
1/2 cup sunflower oil

4 eggs
1 lb (500 g) filo dough
Egg yolk

*Banitsa* is the queen of Bulgarian cuisine. The most popular version uses a filling of white cheese (feta cheese) and eggs. If you travel to Bulgaria, you can try variations of this dish with different fillings: pumpkin and sugar (*tikvenik*), cabbage (*zelnik pie*), onion, spinach, and rice (*klin*) (from the Rhodope Mountains), meat, and others. Another type of *banitsa* uses milk, eggs, and vanilla, and is served as a dessert. The popular dessert *baklava* is also a type of sweet *banitsa*.

**STEPS:**
Preheat oven to 375˚F (190˚C).

**Make Filling**
➢ Crumble the feta cheese and mix it with the yogurt.
➢ Add the oil and mix well.
➢ Stir in the eggs and make sure the mixture is consistent.

**Prepare Dough**
➢ Flatten the package of filo dough sheets and using a brush or a spoon, sprinkle a small amount of oil or butter onto the top sheet and smear it around.
➢ Add a spoonful of the filling and spread it evenly over the entire sheet.
➢ Roll the top two sheets into a log and arrange the log onto the outer edge of a round baking pan that has been greased with butter or oil.
➢ Continue making more logs and place them in the pan in the shape of a spiral until you have used all the filling and the pan is filled.
➢ Mix one yolk with a few drops of water and coat the *banitsa* with it.

**Final Steps:** Bake the *banitsa* for about 35 min. or until the crust is golden. After baking, cut the *banitsa* into pieces. You can eat it hot or cold. It is usually served with yogurt and can be part of your breakfast or lunch.

**An easy modern *Banitsa* variation:** If you want to make this an appetizer to impress people, use small wonton wrappers. Push a wonton wrapper into the bottom of each of the eight sprayed cups in a muffin tin. Spoon the egg-and-feta-cheese mixture evenly into the wonton wrappers. Bake for 18 - 20 minutes until golden brown. Let cool 5 minutes before removing from the muffin tin. For a richer taste, add spinach or ham to the feta cheese mixture. In the end, you will have a variety of appetizers.

# Katmi

| | |
|---|---|
| Package of yeast | 4 cups (1 liter) milk |
| 1/2 cup warm water | 3 eggs |
| 1/2 teaspoon salt | 4 cups (0.5 kg) all purpose flour |
| 1 teaspoon sugar | 1 egg yolk |
| | Butter or cooking spray |

*Katmi* are similar to pancakes, but they are cooked on a special shallow clay or copper pan. In most places in Bulgaria, they are prepared without eggs.

**STEPS:**
Cook on a burner on top of the stove.

**Prepare Batter**
➤ Mix a package of yeast with warm water.
➤ Add salt and sugar.
➤ Mix well and let the yeast dissolve.
➤ Pour milk into another bowl and add the eggs.
➤ Slightly beat the eggs with a spoon until they are a liquid consistency.
➤ Stir in the yeast until it is mixed throughout the egg batter.
➤ Add flour a little at a time and stir in the mixture until it thickens.
➤ Set the batter aside at room temperature or in the oven to allow it time to rise. Bubbles will appear on the surface when it is ready.

**Cook Batter**
➤ Preheat the frying pan on medium heat, or use a flat crêpe pan or cast iron pan.
➤ Separate an egg yolk into a small bowl, and slightly beat it with a spoon.
➤ Coat the pan with butter or olive oil cooking spray.
➤ Pour the stirred yolk over it.
➤ Pour a heaping spoonful of the *katmi* batter onto the pan. Move slowly to cover the bottom of the pan equally. It will form a shape similar to a crêpe. Turn the *katmi* over
➤ with a spatula when the top bubbles or shows holes (only a few seconds). Cook until the other side turns brown.

**Toppings:** When the *katmi* are ready, pour melted butter over them. Then spread on jam or honey, and sprinkle nuts on top. You can roll them up like crêpes, or layer them like a cake, with a filling of your choice in between the layers. Serve them warm, or cold like an appetizer.

# *Patatnik*

| | |
|---|---|
| *2 lbs (1 kg) potatoes* | *2 Tablespoons melted butter* |
| *1 egg* | *Onion* |
| *7 oz (200 g) feta cheese* | *Green peppers (optional)* |
| *Parsley or mint* | *Mushrooms (optional)* |
| *Pinch of salt* | *Ham (optional)* |
| *Black pepper based on your taste* | *1 Tablespoon cooking oil* |

*Patatnik* is a slow-cooked potato dish from the Rhodope Mountains region. It is a simple meal made with grated potatoes, onions, salt, and *gyosum* mint. Other non-traditional ingredients you can use are white cheese (*sirene*) or eggs, in addition to savory and peppers. I sometimes add mushrooms and bits of ham to make it a complete meal. This version uses feta cheese, but you can use any type you like: provolone, white American, etc. Serve warm and enjoy a taste of the Balkans.

**STEPS:**

**Prepare Ingredients**
- Peel and grate the raw potatoes. Set them aside in a spaghetti drainer to remove the potato juice.
- Grate the feta cheese in a small bowl.
- Take a handful of the grated potatoes and with both hands squeeze them to remove extra juice, and then put them in another bowl.
- Repeat the above step until you have all the potatoes in the bowl.
- Stir in the grated feta and the egg.
- Add the parsley (or mint), salt, black pepper, and melted butter.
- Stir until well mixed.
- Chop and add the onion.
- Chop and add the green peppers, mushrooms, and ham (optional).

**Final Steps:** Pour cooking oil in a large, deep skillet (nonstick or cast-iron is best). Turn heat to low. When it's hot, pour in a thin layer of the batter. Shake the pan occasionally, and adjust the heat so the batter doesn't burn. Cook until the bottom is nicely browned, at least 15 minutes. Turn the *patanik* over by sliding it out onto a plate then covering it with another large plate. Invert the plates and slide the *patatnik* back into the pan. Add more oil as necessary. Cook until it becomes golden on the other side. You can also bake it in the oven. Preheat to 375˚F (190˚C). Generously butter an oven-proof dish. Pour the potato mixture into it and bake about 30 - 40 minutes, or until the potatoes are tender. Sprinkle with parsley and grated cheese. Serve warm.

# Sarmi

1 (16 oz) jar grape leaves
2 - 3 carrots
2 onions
1 cup vegetable oil
1 cup of rice
1/2 lb (500 g) ground beef

1/2 cup water
Pinch of sea salt
Paprika, dill, parsley
1 teaspoon chopped garlic
1 stick of butter
2 - 3 cups of water

Traditionally in Bulgaria, *sarmi*, or stuffed grape leaves, are served with yogurt (seasoned with garlic and salt), or you can cover them with *béchamel* (a white sauce made from butter, flour, and milk).

## STEPS:

Preheat oven to 350˚F (190˚C). Cover the bottom of a pot with small pieces of cabbage or grape leaves. It's better to use a clay pot with a cover, and cook the *sarmi* on low heat.

### Prepare Ingredients
➤ Drain the grape leaves and carefully pull them apart.
➤ Finely chop carrots and onions.
➤ Heat a frying pan on low heat and add the vegetable oil.
➤ Add the carrots, onions, rice, and ground beef to the heated oil and stir.
➤ Pour in 1/2 cup of water.
➤ Add salt, paprika, dill, parsley, and garlic to taste, and stir.
➤ Cover and boil on low heat until the rice is swollen, but not fully cooked.

### Fill the Grape Leaves
➤ Place the grape leaves on a flat surface, and add a spoonful of the mixture.
➤ Wrap the leaves into a log.

### Fill Clay Pot
➤ Place the *sarmi* on top of the pieces of grape leaves in the clay pot.
➤ Cut butter into small pieces, add to the pot, and sprinkle with dill and parsley.
➤ Slowly add 2 - 3 cups of water (enough to cover the *sarmi*).
➤ Hold down the *sarmi* with a plate so they don't unwrap.

**Final Step:** Cover the pot and cook for 30 - 35 minutes.

**Variations:** You can use fresh cabbage leaves or sauerkraut instead of grape leaves. If you want to add more flavor, add 2 - 3 crushed walnuts to the stuffing. Cover the *sarmi* with chicken broth rather than water. If you don't want to cover the *sarmi* with a plate, you can simmer them at 200˚F (95˚C) for about an hour.

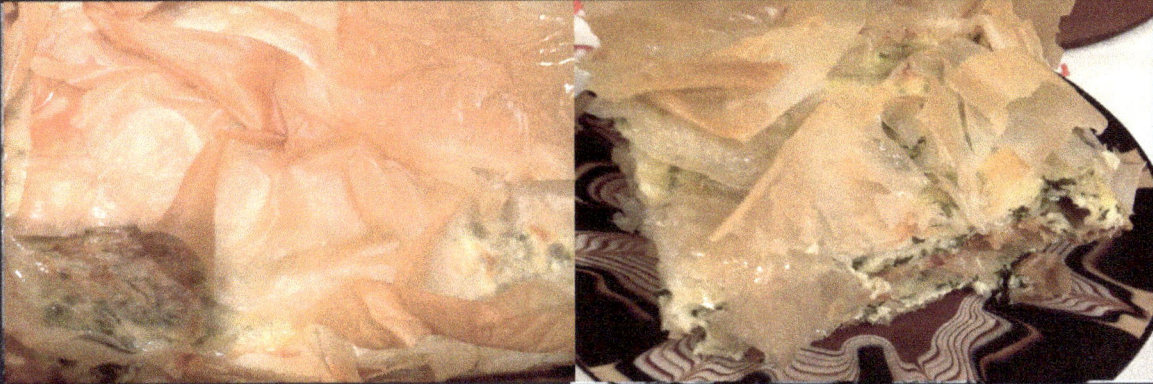

# Rhodopean Klin

*1 lb (500 g) feta cheese*
*1 cup boiled white rice*
*1 lb (500 g) fresh or frozen spinach*
*1/2 cup sunflower oil*

*4 eggs*
*1 lb (500 g) filo dough*
*Egg yolk*

The Rhodope Mountain region, homeland of Orpheus, is one of the most beautiful places in Bulgaria. Its people treat you with hospitality. *Klin* is a specialty *banitsa* from this region. It is deliciously warming and easy to make, proof that simple things are often the best. The filling is made with rice and spinach. Alternate ingredients are kale or other greens according to your mood, creativity, and the season.

**STEPS:**
Preheat oven to 375°F (190°C).

**Prepare Filling**
➢ Crumble the feta cheese and mix it with the rice and spinach.
➢ Add the oil and mix well.
➢ Stir in the eggs and make sure the mixture is consistent.

**Prepare *Klin***
➢ Flatten the filo dough, removing 8 sheets to cover the bottom of a shallow baking pan. The pastry should overlap the edges.
➢ Gently smear the top sheet with oil or butter.
➢ Spread the filling evenly over the sheets using a spoon.
➢ Take another 8 sheets and cover the filling and fold over the top.
➢ Gently sprinkle with oil or butter.
➢ Mix 1 egg yolk with a few drops of water and coat the *klin*.

**Final Steps:** Bake for 35 min. or until it looks golden. For best results, bake for 20 minutes, take the pan out of the oven and turn it upside down on a plate. Flip the entire *klin* over so that it lands in the pan, the opposite side up. Cook for another 20 minutes. After baking, cut the *klin* into pieces.

**Variation - Versatile *Klin* wontons:** To make an appetizer, use small wonton wrappers. This quick recipe makes a great crunchy afternoon snack or a meal when paired with a bowl of soup on a cold winter day. Position the wonton wrapper with one point toward you. Place 2 spoonfuls of filling in the center of the wrapper. Fold the bottom corner over the filling. Fold the sides toward the center over the filling. Roll toward the remaining point (shape of a log). Moisten the top corner with water or egg yolk and press to seal. Repeat with remaining wrappers and filling. Place on baking sheets coated with oil. Lightly coat wontons with oil or butter and yolk. Bake at 375°F (190°C) for 15 - 20 minutes or until golden brown, turning once.

**www.mysticalemona.com**

# Zucchini with Yogurt

1/2 cup plain yogurt
2 teaspoons chopped fresh dill
1 small clove garlic, grated
1/2 teaspoon lemon juice

Salt
Freshly ground black pepper
1 lb (500 g) zucchini
1 teaspoon olive oil

Bulgaria produces more than 100 varieties of yogurt. Not only is it eaten plain, it is used when cooking or preparing many dishes. It is no wonder, since yogurt was invented by the Thracians, a fact about which Bulgarians are proud. From a cold drink during the summer to a hot lunch, yogurt is certain to be an ingredient.

**STEPS:**
Cook under broiler.

**Prepare Dill Mixture**
➤ In a small bowl, whisk together the yogurt, dill, garlic, and lemon juice. If necessary add a few drops of water to make the mixture of pourable consistency.
➤ Season to taste with salt and a pinch of black pepper.
➤ Set aside.

**Prepare Zucchini**
➤ Trim the ends off the zucchini and cut it into thin slices or strips (circles or long strips).
➤ Toss with olive oil, salt, and pepper.
➤ Place the zucchini in an oven-proof skillet or pan and broil, flipping occasionally, about 10 minutes until slightly charred and tender, but not mushy.

**Final Steps:** Remove from broiler. Serve zucchini warm or chilled, covered or dipped in the yogurt-dill sauce.

**Alternatives:** If you want a richer taste, coat the zucchini with flour. Place the pieces (circles or strips) into a frying pan with about a half inch of heated oil. Fry the zucchini pieces until they are golden brown and crispy. In the summer, you can use a grill instead.

**Other Yogurt Ideas**
*Tarator* - Bulgarian Cold Cucumber Soup.
*Airan* - a drink made of yogurt, cold water, and salt.

For more great ideas, check Maria's Kitchen page on MysticalEmona.com.

# Thracian Guvetch

*Savory and fresh parsley*
*1 onion*
*1/2 lb mushrooms*
*2 tomatoes*
*1/2 lb feta cheese*
*Cooking oil*

*Chili powder*
*Black pepper (or hot peppers)*
*1/2 lb smoked or precooked*
*   chorizo sausage*
*1/4 cup grated cheese*
*2 eggs*

One of the tastiest Bulgarian cuisines is a meal prepared in a clay pot (*guvetch*). Bulgaria has as many variations of the *guvetch* as it does regions. Throughout the centuries, people adapted the recipe by using available ingredients. Every time my mother made this dish, it was different and more delicious than the last time. Cooking it in the *guvetch* was the reason. The pot itself is quite colorful, a piece of art. Bulgarian ceramics are unique and the designs are full of imagination. A classic type of Bulgarian pottery is called *Troyan*. If you don't have a *guvetch*, you can use any type of clay cooking pot. The idea is to experiment and discover different flavors to enhance your food.

**STEPS:**
Preheat oven to 420°F (215°C).

**Prepare the Ingredients**
➤ Chop the parsley, onion, mushrooms, and tomatoes.
➤ Slice the feta cheese into tiles.

**Fill the *Guvetch***
➤ Pour a little cooking oil into the pot and place some onion on top.
➤ Arrange lines of feta cheese, then mushrooms, then tomatoes, and the remaining onion.
➤ Sprinkle with parsley and savory.
➤ Add chili powder and black pepper or whole hot peppers if you prefer to cook with them.
➤ Arrange the sausage on top. If you can't find chorizo, you can use any kind of precooked or cured smoked sausage.
➤ Cover the pot and place it in the oven.
➤ Bake for 15 - 20 minutes.
➤ Remove the lid and sprinkle with grated cheese.
➤ Crack both eggs on top and bake for another 10 - 15 minutes.

**Final Steps:** Remove from the oven and sprinkle with fresh parsley. Combine with a glass of red wine and enjoy the taste of Bulgaria and the Balkans.

# Tikvenik

| | |
|---|---|
| 1 1/2 lbs (680 g) pumpkin or butternut squash | Honey |
| 1 cup sugar (or brown sugar) | 1/2 lb butter (2 sticks), melted (optional) |
| 1 teaspoon ground cinnamon | 1 lb (500 g) filo dough |
| 2 oz (55 g) chopped walnuts | 2 - 3 Tablespoons powdered sugar (for sprinkling on top) |

*Tikvenik* is a sweet pumpkin *banitsa* made mostly in the fall and winter months. It is a common food served on *Koleda* and *Budni vecher*.

**STEPS:**
Preheat oven to 350˚F (190˚C).

**Make Filling**
➤ Mix together the sugar, cinnamon, and walnuts in a small bowl.
➤ Cut the pumpkin or squash into large chunks and grate it.
➤ Add the walnut mixture to the grated pumpkin/squash.
➤ Add a few drops of honey.
➤ Pour the melted butter over the pumpkin/squash mixture.

**Prepare Dough**
➤ Open the package of filo dough and spread it out.
➤ Cut it horizontally and vertically into 4 equal pieces.
➤ Remove 2 sheets from one pile and place the filo with a point facing you.
➤ Sprinkle vegetable oil or melted butter over it (not more than a teaspoon).
➤ Spread 2 - 3 Tablespoons of the pumpkin/squash mixture evenly over the filo (so it slightly covers the surface).
➤ Sprinkle some of the leftover sugar on top of that.
➤ Fold the corner facing you over the filling, then fold the two sides over that.
➤ Roll the filo toward the remaining point so it is shaped like a log.
➤ Place the log on a greased baking dish, with the open end down.
➤ Repeat the process until all the filling is used.
➤ Sprinkle vegetable oil over the top, coating the filo so it doesn't become dry.

**Final Steps:** Bake for about 20 - 30 min. until the filo is crispy and golden on top. Remove from the pan immediately after baking and let it cool. Sprinkle lightly with powdered sugar.

**Variation:** If you don't like pumpkin or squash, use apples instead. Make sure to drain some of the juice from the apples, but not all of it. Before you bake it, sprinkle grated apple and nuts over each piece to add a little bit of a twist.

# Rhodope Baked Beans

14 oz (400 g) of white kidney beans
2 onions
1 carrot
Celery
3 - 4 Tablespoons vegetable oil
3 - 4 Tablespoons flour

Red pepper to taste
2 tomatoes, grated
Savory, mint
Smoked sausages
1 package pizza dough

This is a variation of a famous recipe for *Smilian* beans, named after a town in the Rhodope Mountains. There is even a Bean Museum there. This hearty meal of beans topped with fresh baked bread is perfect for a long, cold winter day.

**STEPS:**
Preheat oven to 375°F (190°C) after beans are cooked.

**Prepare Beans**
➤ Put the beans in a pot of water and leave to soak for about 12 hours.
➤ Drain the water and add fresh water.
➤ Bring it to a complete boil, then lower the heat to medium.
➤ Slice one onion, a carrot, and some celery.
➤ Add them to the boiling beans.
➤ When the beans are soft, turn the heat low and let them simmer.

**Prepare Bean Bullion**
➤ Put 3 - 4 spoonfuls of vegetable oil into a frying pan, and turn on low heat.
➤ Chop the second onion and put it into the heated oil.
➤ Cook until it gets soft and a little clear.
➤ Sprinkle it with flour and red pepper.
➤ Stir occasionally.
➤ Once the flour and onions are cooked, add 1 scoop of beans.
➤ Mash and fry them for a short time only, so the flour doesn't burn.
➤ Grate the tomatoes and mix them until they form a smooth paste.
➤ Pour the tomato paste onto the beans in the frying pan and let it boil until the beans are cooked.

**Final Steps:** After the beans are cooked, preheat the oven and fill 4 clay French onion soup bowls (or any clay pot) with beans and add a little of the bean bullion until they are half full. Add savory and mint. Cut up some sausages and add them. Fill the clay pot up to the cover line. If you have time, make biscuit dough from scratch. Otherwise, use ready-to-bake pizza dough and make 4 "caps" to cover each clay pot. Leave the pots until the dough rises. Bake about 35 minutes until the dough is cooked. Remove the pots and let them cool off a little.

# Easy Baklava

| | |
|---|---|
| 1 package puff pastry shells (6 shells) | 1/2 cup white sugar |
| 1/2 teaspoon ground cinnamon | 1/2 cup water |
| 1/2 cup chopped mixed nuts | 1 teaspoon honey |
| 1/2 cup butter, melted | 1/2 teaspoon vanilla extract |
| | 1/2 teaspoon grated lemon zest |

*Baklava* is a well-known dessert served not only on *Koleda* and *Survaki*, but also throughout the year. The dessert was listed in a thirteenth century Turkish cookbook. The following is a modern recipe I invented that saves time and hassle.

**STEPS:**
Preheat oven to 385˚F (200˚C).

**Prepare Shells**
➢ Butter a round shallow baking dish.
➢ Toss together cinnamon and nuts in a small bowl.
➢ Break open a package of pastry puffs along the pre-scored lines to separate the shells. Take them out of the freezer at least 4 - 5 hours prior to baking.
➢ Place the puffs onto the baking sheet with their tops up.
➢ Brush them generously with melted butter.
➢ Sprinkle 2 - 3 Tablespoons of the nut mixture on top.
➢ Bake for 20 minutes, until puffs rise and are crisp and golden.

**Prepare Syrup**
➢ While the puffs are baking, combine the sugar and water in a small saucepan over medium heat and bring to a boil.
➢ Stir in the honey, vanilla, and lemon zest.
➢ Reduce the heat and simmer for 30 minutes.

**Final Steps:** Remove the puffs from the oven and let them cool for 15 - 20 minutes. Spoon the syrup over them. Let them cool completely before serving. Store uncovered. The best way to bring out the flavor of *baklava* is to let it cool for about 24 hours. When it is dry, make an additional syrup mixture and spoon it over the top of the puffs.

**Variation:** Use puff pastry sheets. Spread the nut mixture onto a sheet, patting it down with your hands. Sprinkle melted butter on top. Start rolling the log from the filled edge until you have a firm even log. Using a sharp or serrated knife, cut the log into 1/2 inch slices. Place them on a waxed-paper lined tray. Preheat oven to 385˚F (200˚C). Bake for about 15 - 20 minutes or until golden brown. Prepare the syrup and the rest of the recipe as described above.

# Koledna Pitka

| | |
|---|---|
| *1 package yeast* | *4 cups (1 kg) flour* |
| *1 teaspoon sugar* | *4 cups (1 liter) water* |
| *1 cup (1/4 liter) lukewarm water* | *Walnuts* |
| *1 teaspoon salt* | *Dried fruit* |

*Koledna Pitka*, or fortune bread, is the most important part of the meal on *Budni vecher*. It is a round loaf of bread with a coin and possibly fortunes inside. The top is decorated with dough, either religious symbols or ones representing the family occupation (birds, cross, letters, plough, sheep, and so on). In some regions, it is decorated with dry fruit and walnuts.

**STEPS:**
Preheat oven to 375°F (190°C) after the dough has risen.

**Prepare Starter Dough**
➢ Add the yeast and sugar to a large mixing bowl.
➢ Pour the lukewarm water over the yeast and sugar to dissolve them.
➢ When dissolved, stir the mixture with a spoon.
➢ Slowly add half a cup of flour, stirring it until well mixed.
➢ Let the yeast mixture rise.

**Knead the Dough**
➢ Sift the remaining flour together with the salt.
➢ Pour the flour into a large round pan and form a "well" in the middle.
➢ When the starter dough rises to twice its original size, put it into the well.
➢ Stir it with a spoon at first to mix with the flour, then afterwards knead it with floured hands.
➢ Slowly add 4 cups of lukewarm water, kneading the dough into the flour as you do this until all the flour has been mixed into the dough.
➢ Put the dough on a greased tray and cover with a cloth.
➢ Let it rise in a warm place until it is double in size.

**Final Steps:** While waiting for the dough to rise, write fortunes on a few small pieces of paper. I usually do one for each member in the house or dinner party. When done, roll each fortune in foil. Wrap a coin in foil as well. When the dough has risen, knead it once again and spread it carefully in a baking pan. Distribute the fortunes equally throughout the dough. Decorate the dough with walnuts and dried fruit. Put the pan into a preheated oven to bake.

At the dinner table, break the bread and give each person a piece. Make sure to leave the first piece on a plate. This is the fortune for the entire household. Enjoy your fresh bread and have a great and prosperous new year.

# Lazy Koledna Pitka

*2 loaves frozen dough*
*1 egg*
*1/2 cup feta cheese crumbs*

Since we are all busy and time is the only thing we are short off nowadays, the following variation to *Koledna Pitka* is my version of the bread in a modern and easy-to-do style.

**STEPS:**
Preheat oven to 375°F (190°C).

**Prepare First Loaf**
➢ Leave the frozen dough at room temperature until it gets soft.
➢ Spread oil in a baking pan to prevent the dough from sticking to the sides.
➢ Place one loaf in the pan. I like to use a round baking pan, not a shallow one, so the dough doesn't overflow the edge when it rises.
➢ With kitchen scissors, cut the loaf into small thin strips.

**Add Fortunes**
➢ Write fortunes on a few small pieces of paper. I usually do one for each member in the house or dinner party. When done, roll each fortune in foil. Wrap a coin in foil as well.
➢ Insert the coin and fortunes into the dough.

**Prepare Second Loaf**
➢ Mix the egg and feta cheese crumbs together and spread evenly over the top of the loaf.
➢ Cut the second loaf into small pieces and place them over the first one, covering the feta-cheese mixture.
➢ Sprinkle with feta cheese or use grated cheese, the same as what is used for pizza.
➢ Cover the pan and let the dough rise at room temperature or near the warming oven until it has doubled in size.
➢ Bake for 30 - 35 minutes.
➢ Let it cool near the oven for another 30 minutes.

Voila! Here is the lazy Bulgarian's *pitka* baked with love!

# References

*Internet links change frequently. These were valid at the time we did our research.*

**Budni Vecher**

Bezovska, Albena and Konstantinova, Daniela (trans.), "Christmas Eve, a major family occasion," Dec. 10, 2012. http://bnr.bg/en/post/100179166/christmas-eve-a-major-family-occasion.

Doser.org. "Ancient Christmas traditions in Bulgaria - Budni vecher." http://doser.org/bulgaria/koleda.htm.

English staff. "Ignazhden (St. Ingatius' day), folk-wise." Dec. 16, 2009. http://bnr.bg/en/post/100099910/ignazhden-st-ingatius-day-folk-wise.

HostingUK.com. "The Bulgarian Festival Calendar - KOLEDA (Christmas)." http://12121.hostinguk.com/Koleda.htm.

Konstantinova, Daniela (trans.). "Christmas Eve." Dec. 17, 2011. http://bnr.bg/en/post/100133263/christmas-eve.

Plovdiv Guide. "Badni Vecher (Christmas Eve) - December 24." http://www.plovdivguide.com/_m1703/Traditions-Namedays/BADNI-VECHER-CHRISTMAS-EVE---December-24-605.

**Survaki**

Art on the Move. "Survachka." artonthemove.wikispaces.com/file/view/SURVACHKA.doc.

Dikanarova, Margarita. "Cornel-tree twig, wild-geranium posy and ritual loaf of bread in Christmas and New Year traditions." Dec. 19, 2009. http://bnr.bg/en/post/100100132/cornel-tree-twig-wild-geranium-posy-and-ritual-loaf-of-bread-in-christmas-and-new-year-traditions.

Konstantinova, Daniela. "With the New Year knocking on the door: about borderlines, gratitude and expectations." Dec. 19, 2013. http://bnr.bg/en/post/100276604/with-the-new-year-knocking-on-the-door-about-borderlines-gratitude-and-expectations

Petcova, Rossitsa (trans.). "Traditional beliefs related to tree symbolism." June 29, 2011. http://bnr.bg/en/post/100124014/traditional-beliefs-related-to-tree-symbolism.

Serafimov, Pavel. "Surva, Bulgarian Sourvakars Divine Light" (translated). Dec. 29, 2014. http://sparotok.blogspot.com/2014/12/blog-post_29.html?m=1.

**Trifonovden**

Admin. "The Thracian Community." July 29, 2014. http://freesofiatour.com/blog/the-thracian-community.

Athanassakis, Apostolos N. (trans.) and Wolkow, Benjamin M. (trans.). The Orphic Hymns. Baltimore, MD: The Johns Hopkins University Press, 2013.

English staff. "The symbolic meaning of wine." Feb. 9, 2010. http://bnr.bg/en/post/100102283/the-symbolic-meaning-of-wine.

English staff. "Trifon Zarezan (St. Trifon the Pruner), folk-wise." Feb. 12, 2010. http://bnr.bg/en/post/100102483/trifon-zarezan-st-trifon-the-pruner-folk-wise.

Godwin, Joscelyn, Ph.D. "The Orphic Mysteries." In The Golden Thread. Quest Books, the imprint of the Theosophical Publishing House, 2007. https://www.rosicrucian.org/publications/digest/digest1_2008/11_Godwin_The%20Orphic%20Mysteries/ONLINE_11_Godwin.pdf.

GreekMythology.com. "Dionysus." http://www.greekmythology.com/Other_Gods/Dionysus/dionysus.html.

Gross, Rachel and Grote, Dale. "Dionysus." Encyclopedia Mythica™. http://www.pantheon.org/articles/d/dionysus.html.

Petcova, Rossitsa (trans.). "Fifty heroes are drinking wine, or about grapes and wine in Bulgarian folklore." Feb. 14, 2013. http://bnr.bg/en/post/100186573/fifty-heroes-are-drinking-wine-or-about-grapes-and-wine-in-bulgarian-folklore.

Petcova, Rossitsa (trans.). "Folk songs about vine growing and wine making." Feb. 15, 2011. http://bnr.bg/en/post/100118217/folk-songs-about-vine-growing-and-wine-making.

Petcova, Rossitsa (trans.). "Saint Trifon's Day." Feb. 13, 2012. http://bnr.bg/en/post/100140649/saint-trifons-day.

Vazkresenska, Minka. "Saint Trifon Who?" http://www.eurochicago.com/2011/02/saint-trifon-who/.

Villa Yustina. "Thracians and wine." http://villayustina.com/index.php?option=com_content&view=article&id=

33%3Ahistory&catid=6%3Aaboutus&Itemid=1&lang=en.

## Baba Marta Den

Az-jenata.bg. "Do you know when you need to take off the martenitsa?" (translated.) March 2, 2014. http://www.az-jenata.bg/a/8-svobodno-vreme/3647-koga-se-svalyat-martenitzite/.

Bezovska. Albena and Markov, Alexander (trans.). "Granny Marta and her brothers." Feb. 28, 2011. http://bnr.bg/en/post/100118844/granny-marta-and-her-brothers.

Ganeva, Dr. Radoslava. "Bulgarian Folk Costumes – Symbols and Traditions." Bulgarian Diplomatic Review, Supplement to Issue 3/2003, Year 3.

Harizanova, Tania and Konstantinova, Daniela (trans.). "Martenitsa, the uniquely Bulgarian symbol Granny Martha: what a lovely feast!" http://bnr.bg/en/post/100336855/martenitsa-the-uniquely-bulgarian-symbol.

HostingUK.com. "The Bulgarian Festival Calendar - Granny Martha's Day." http://12121.hostinguk.com/martenitsa.htm.

Intangible Cultural Heritage. "Martenitsa." http://www.unesco-bg.org/culture/bul-ich/?language=us&article=documents& section=ich&post=17.

Mandeville, Terry M. "Baba Marta Day & The Martenitsa." 2008. http://www.orgsites.com/wa/facab/_pgg7.php3#C4.

Panayotova, Rumyana and Konstantinova, Daniela (trans.). "March 1, Granny Martha rites." Feb. 26, 2010. http://bnr.bg/en/post/100103127/march-1-granny-martha-rites.

PaylessBG.com. "Traditions and Customs of Bulgaria." http://www. paylessbg.com/en/articles/Traditions-and-Customs-of-Bulgaria/11/.

Petcova, Rossitsa (trans.) "Cold winter and heavy snow in Bulgarian folklore." Feb. 22, 2013. http://bnr.bg/en/post/100187648/cold-winter-and-heavy-snow-in-bulgarian-folklore.

Petcova, Rossitsa (trans.). "March 1 is one of Bulgaria's best-loved holidays." March 1, 2011. http://bnr.bg/en/post/100118915/march-1-is-one-of-bulgarias-best-loved-holidays.

Rossier, Darina. "1st of March, Martenitsa and Baba Martha." http://www.learn-bulgarian.net/blog/1st-of-march-martenitsi-and-baba-martha/.

Ruseva, Rositsa. "Legend of the Martenitsa in Bulgaria." http://www.topics-mag.com/edition26/bulgaria/martenitsa.html.

Sheehan, Moni and Armstrong, Paraskeva (trans.). "Why March has 31 Days." From "A Spell in Time." https://www.h-net.org/~nilas/seasons/march31.htm.

## Sirni Zagovezni

Bezovska, Albena and Konstantinova, Daniela (trans.). "Shrovetide first Sunday before Lent." Feb. 26, 2011. https://bnr.bg/en/post/100118780/shrovetide-first-sunday-before-lent.

Petcova, Rossitsa (trans.). "Orthodoxy and pagan rites on Forgiveness Sunday." Feb. 24, 2012. http://bnr.bg/en/post/100142466/orthodoxy-and-pagan-rites-on-forgiveness-sunday.

Regional Museum Burgas. "Mesni and Sirni Zagovezni." http://www.burgasmuseums.bg/index.php?tab=ethno&lang=en&page=encyc&enc=rituals&eid=70.

## Kukerovden

Bakalova, Kalina (Under the Direction of Freda Scott Giles). "Kukeri: Ritual Performances in Bulgaria." https://getd.libs.uga.edu/pdfs/bakalova_kalina_p_200905_phd.pdf. Athens, GA: The University of Georgia, 2009.

European Virtual Museum. "Pagan Rites Connected with the Winter Solstice." http://europeanvirtualmuseum.net/evm/vm/deepening/popup_12_en.htm.

Fol, Valeria. "The kouker without mask: The masquerade feasts in Southeastern Europe," Orpheus, in "Journal of Indo-European and Thracian Studies." Vol. 7, 1977. Institute of Thracolgoy, pp. 83 – 99.

Lirael. "Discover Bulgaria: Kukeri." May 12, 2013. http://lirael.blog.co. uk/2013/05/12/discover-bulgaria-kukeri-15958740/.

Mishkova, Iglika. "Dreaming of Mummers/Survashkari." https://www.academia.edu/10066480/Dreaming_of_Mummers_Survashkari.

Modern Rodnovery. "Ringing in the Spring: The Old Slavic Carnival." http://modrodnovery.com/2014/02/05/zvancari-ring-in-the-spring-the-old-slavic-carnival/.

Petcova, Rossitsa (trans.). "Orthodoxy and pagan rites on Forgiveness Sunday. Feb. 23, 2012. http://bnr.bg/en/post/ 100142466/orthodoxy-and-pagan-rites-on-forgiveness-sunday.

Scribol. "The Kukeri Ritual: Bulgaria's Sinister Day of Monsters." http://scribol.com/anthropology-and-history/the-kukeri-ritual-bulgarias-sinister-day-of-monsters/0.

## Todorovden

Bezovska, Albena and Popova, Vyara (trans.). "The Horse, mediator between the netherworld and the Earth." March 13, 2011. https://bnr.bg/en/post/100119361/the-horse-mediator-between-the-netherworld-and-the-earth.

Dikanarova, Margarita (trans.). "St. Todor's Day." Feb. 18, 2010. https://bnr.bg/en/post/100102723/st-todors-day.

HostingUK.com. "The Bulgarian Festival Calendar - Saint Todor's Day (Saint Theodore's Day)." http://12121 .hostinguk.com/todor.htm.

Perry Carolyn. "Bulgarian tumulus reveals Thracian tribal ruler buried with his horses." Aug. 12, 2014. http://carolynperry.blogspot.com/2014/08/thracian-burial-reveals-tribal-ruler.html.

Quest Bulgaria. "St. Todor's Day." http://www.questbg.com/www. questbg.com/lifestyle/life/1521-st-todors-day.html.

## Blagovets

Admin. "The Thracian Community." July 29, 2014. http://freesofiatour.com/blog/the-thracian-community.

Bezovska, Albena and Petcova, Rossitsa (trans.). "Beliefs and rituals related to snakes and cuckoos." March 16, 2012. http://bnr.bg/en/post/100145675/beliefs-and-rituals-related-to-snakes-and-cuckoos.

Bulgaria today. "Fairies wreak terror in the Elena Balkan, Vanga warned them." (translated). Feb. 7, 2013. http://www.24chasa.bg/Article.asp?ArticleId=1759771.

Goddessrealm. "Vila Goddess of Transformation." http://goddessrealm. com/component/content/article/3-goddess/15-vila-goddess-of-transformation.

HostingUK.com. "The Bulgarian Festival Calendar - Blagovets – Blagostina (The Annunciation)." http://12121 .hostinguk.com/annunciation.htm.

Ilieva, Dr. Angelina and Konstantinova, Daniela (trans.). "Storks and Swallows." April 6, 2012. http://bnr.bg/en/ post/100148557/storks-and-swallows.

Konstantinova, Daniela (trans.). "The serpent in traditional culture: a lethal enemy, a magical helper." Oct. 16, 2013. http://bnr.bg/en/post/100217201/the-serpent-in-traditional-culture-a-lethal-enemy-a-magical-helper.

Kraev, Georg and Petcova, Rossitsa (trans.). "The Day of the Annunciation in Bulgarian folklore." March 25, 2012. http://bnr.bg/sites/en/Lifestyle/Folklore/Pages/AnnunciationBlagovestenie.aspx.

Milkova, Stiliana. "Walled-in Wives, Dragon's Brides, and Wild Fairies: Women in the Bulgarian Folk Tradition." In Forum Folkloristika, Eastern European Folklife Center. Inaugural Edition. Issue 1, Spring 2012. https://www.eefc.org/folkloristika_1-1.shtml.

Novinite.com. "Unique Thracian Symbol of Royalty Discovered in Bulgaria." June 11, 2007. http://www.novinite .com/view_news.php?id=81728/.

Petcova, Rossitsa (trans.). "Traditional beliefs related to tree symbolism." June 29, 2011. http://bnr.bg/en/post/ 100124014/traditional-beliefs-related-to-tree-symbolism.

Rossier, Darina. "Bulgarian Folklore: Samodiva." http://www.learn-bulgarian.net/blog/bulgarian-folklore-samodiva/.

Samovila on Tumblr. "Samodiva/Samovila & Yuda." May 21, 2012. http://samovila.tumblr.com/post/ 23481149711/samodiva-samovila-yuda.

## Lazarovden

Bezovska, Albena and Konstantinova, Daniela (trans.). "Lazaritsa and Tsvetnisa." April 12, 2014. https://bnr.bg/en/ post/100385512/lazaritsa-and-tsvetnisa.

BulgariaTravel.org. "Traditions, Crafts, and Ethnography. Lazaruvane (St. Lazar's Day Songs and Dances)." http://bulgariatravel. org/data/doc/eng_24-lazaruvane.pdf.

Ganeva, Dr. Radoslava. "Bulgarian Folk Costumes – Symbols and Traditions." Bulgarian Diplomatic Review, Supplement to Issue 3/2003, Year 3.

Markov, Alexander (trans.). "Dragons and Lamias in Bulgarian folklore." May 31, 2013. https://bnr.bg/en/post/ 100200249/dragons-and-lamias-in-bulgarian-folklore.

Milkova, Stiliana. "Walled-in Wives, Dragon's Brides, and Wild Fairies: Women in the Bulgarian Folk Tradition." In Forum Folkloristika, Eastern European Folklife Center. Inaugural Edition. Issue 1, Spring 2012. https://www.eefc.org/folkloristika_1-1.shtml.

Nikov, Nikola. "Holidays of the Bulgarians in Myths and Legends." http://www.promacedonia.org/bg_folklore/en/index.htm.

Panayotova, Rumiana and Petcova Rossitsa (trans.). "Beliefs and superstitions about dragons." May 18, 2012. https://bnr.bg/en/post/100154206/beliefs-and-superstitions-about-dragons.

Petcova, Rossitsa (trans.). "Lazarus Saturday and Palm Sunday – the heralds of Easter." March 26, 2010. https://bnr.bg/en/post/100104417/lazarus-saturday-and-palm-sunday-the-heralds-of-easter.

Petcova, Rossitsa (trans.). "Saint Lazarus Saturday and Palm Sunday in Bulgarian folklore." April 6, 2012. https://bnr.bg/en/post/100148556/saint-lazarus-saturday-and-palm-sunday-in-bulgarian-folklore.

Petcova, Rossitsa (trans.). "Springtime pre-wedding folk rituals." May 16, 2011. https://bnr.bg/en/post/100122119/springtime-pre-wedding-folk-rituals.

## Tsvetnitsa

Popova, Vyara (trans.). "Tsvetnitsa or the Day of Flowers." April 18, 2011. https://bnr.bg/en/post/100120950/tsvetnitsa-or-the-day-of-flowers.

## Velikden

Bezovska, Albena and Daynova, Milena (trans.). "In the beginning was the egg: the tradition of decorated Easter eggs in Bulgaria." April 19, 2014. https://bnr.bg/en/post/100397315/in-the-beginning-was-the-egg-the-tradition-of-decorated-easter-eggs-in-bulgaria.

Harizanova, Tania and Konstantinova, Daniela (trans.). "Easter Mosaic." April 21, 2014. https://bnr.bg/en/post/100397655/easter-mosaic.

Konstantinova, Daniela (trans.). "Easter in Bulgarian Traditions." March 31, 2010. htttp://bnr.bg/en/post/100104632/easter-in-bulgarian-traditions.

Konstantinova, Daniela (trans.). "The egg: symbolic meanings and rituals." April 22, 2014. https://bnr.bg/en/post/100195315/the-egg-symbolic-meanings-and-rituals.

## Kostadinovden

Admin. "The Thracian Community." July 29, 2014. http://freesofiatour.com/blog/the-thracian-community.

Apostolov, Mario. "Strandzha." http://www.unspecial.org/2012/10/strandzha/.

Konstantinova, Daniela (trans.). "Bulgaria presents six new nominations for UNESCO." April 17, 2013. http://bnr.bg/en/post/100194702/bulgaria-presents-six-new-nominations-for-unesco.

Markov, Alexander (trans.). "Between Christmas and New Year's folklore festival took place in Sofia." Dec. 30, 2009. http://bnr.bg/en/post/100100559/between-christmas-and-new-years-folklore-festival-took-place-in-sofia.

Neykova, Ruzha. "Nestinarstvo: On Materials of South-East Bulgaria." https://www.academia.edu/5159119/Nestinarstvo_On_Materials_of_South-East_Bulgaria.

Plovdiv Guide. "Traditions & Name Days - ST. CONSTANTINE AND HELENA - May 21." http://www.plovdivguide.com/_m1703/Traditions-Namedays/ST-ST-CONSTANTINE-AND-HELENA---May-21-532.

Popova, Vyara (trans.). "Nestinarstvo or Bulgarian fire-dancing." May 30, 2011. http://bnr.bg/en/post/100122668/nestinarstvo-or-bulgarian-fire-dancing.

Shivachev, S. "Nistinare." In Svetlina, pp. 1898-9. From Barber, Elizabeth Wayland. Chapter 22, "Nestinari: Bulgarian Firewalkers." http://elizabethwaylandbarber.com/nestinari-bulgarian-firewalkers-chap-22/.

Stanchev, Zhivko (trans.). "Magic ritual of Nestinarstvo in Strandja." May 31, 2012. http://bnr.bg/en/post/100155800/magic-ritual-of-nestinarstvo-in-strandja.

UNESCO. "Nestinarstvo, messages from the past." https://www.youtube. com/watch?v=-ru506gJ1iI.

UNESCO. "Nestinarstvo, messages from the past: the Panagyr of Saints Constantine and Helena in the village of Bulgari." http://www. unesco.org/culture/ich/RL/00191.

**Eniovden**

English staff. "Enio's day /Midsummer day/, June 24th." June 24, 2010. http://bnr.bg/en/post/100108357/.

Journey.bg. "Eniovden - Midsummer Day." http://en.journey.bg/bulgaria/bulgaria.php?guide=377.

Konstantinova, Daniela (trans.). "O Moon, the Sun's bride." Nov. 5, 2013. http://bnr.bg/en/post/100220002/o-moon-the-suns-bride.

Markov, Vassil. "The Ancient Thracian Megalithic Sanctuary 'Markov Kamak' at Tsarev Peak in Rila Mountain: Semantic and Functional Analysis." https://www.academia.edu/3415032/The_Ancient_Thracien_Sanctuary_Markov_kamak_at_Carev_Peak_in_Rila_Mountain_Semantic_and_Functional_Analisis.


**Prokopi Pchelar**

Baeva, Dr. Vihra and Konstantinova, Daniela (trans.). "About bubonic plague and its lords." Jan. 22, 2014. http://bnr.bg/en/post/100183735/about-bubonic-plague-and-its-lords.

Bezovska, Albena and Daynova, Milena (trans.). "Wondrous young lass flying over meadows—bee legends." Feb. 10, 2015. http://bnr.bg/en/post/100519689/wondrous-young-lass-flying-over-meadows-bee-legends.

Bulfinch, Thomas. Bulfinch's Mythology: The Age of Fable or Stories of Gods and Heroes. Chapter 24. http://www.greekmythology.com/Books/Bulfinch/B_Chapter_24/b_chapter_24.html.

Dill, Denise. "Honey: A Spoonful a Day Keeps the Doctor Away!" Sept. 30, 2013, From *Healthy Living*. http://farmersalmanac.com/health/2013/09/30/honey-a-spoonful-a-day-keeps-the-doctor-away/.

Džambov, Vladimir. "St. Great Martyr Procipius." Feb. 2014. http://prablarchive.blogspot.com/2014/02/st-great-martyr-procopius.html.

Fol, Valeria. "Rock-Cut Caves with Two Entrances or the Model of the Cosmos." In *Thracia* 15. pp. 239 – 250. Sofia: Tangra TanNakRa Publishing House, 2003.

Geiling, Natasha. "The Science Behind Honey's Eternal Shelf Life." Aug. 22, 1013. http://www.smithsonianmag.com/science-nature/the-science-behind-honeys-eternal-shelf-life-1218690/#uuTgCSY1FUwYASyq.99.

HostingUK.com. "The Bulgarian Festival Calendar - Saint Procopius: Bee-Keeper's Day July 08." http://12121.hostinguk.com/ProcopiusBEE.htm.

Konstantinova, Daniela (trans.). "Beekeeping and honey in Bulgarian tradition." Feb. 8, 2013. http://bnr.bg/en/post/100185834/beekeeping-and-honey-in-bulgarian-tradition.

Petcova, Rossitsa (trans.). "Bulgarian honey increasingly popular among foreigners." March 28, 2014. http://bnr.bg/en/post/100380602/bulgarian-honey-increasingly-popular-among-foreigners.

Porphyry. Translated by Thomas Taylor. "On the Cave of the Nymphs in the Thirteenth Book of the Odyssey." London: John M. Watkins, 1917. http://www.tertullian.org/fathers/porphyry_cave_of_nymphs_02_translation.htm.

Quote Investigator. "If the Bee Disappeared Off the Face of the Earth, Man Would Only Have Four Years Left To Live." Aug. 27, 2013. http://quoteinvestigator.com/2013/08/27/einstein-bees/.

A Spell in Time. "Bee-Keeper's Day." https://m2.facebook.com/ASpellInTime/photos/a.661510940530147.1073741846.295319337149311/891918507489388/?type=1&refid=17.

Theoi Greek Mythology. "Aristaios." http://www.theoi.com/Georgikos/Aristaios.html.


**Dimitrovden**

Baeva, Vihra. "A Local Cult, a Universal Symbol: The Golden Apple in Gorni Voden, Southern Bulgaria." Our Europe. Ethnography – Ethnology – Anthropology of Culture. Vol. 2/2013, pp. 73-88. http://www.ptpn.poznan.pl/Wydawnictwo/czasopisma/our/OE-2013-073-088-Baeva.pdf.

Bezovska, Albena and Atanasov, Kostadin (trans.). "Details and facts about Bulgarian family services and religious sacrifice." Aug. 31, 2014. http://bnr.bg/en/post/print/100453885/details-and-facts-about-bulgarian-family-services-and-religious-sacrifice.

Bezovska, Albena and Konstantinova, Daniela (trans.). "Dimitrovden, St. Demetrius Feast." Oct. 26, 2014. http://bnr.bg/en/post/100476630/dimitrovden-st-demetrius-feast.

Bezovska, Albena and Konstantinova, Daniela (trans.). "Gergiovden: greenery, lamb and merrymaking." May 6, 2014. http://bnr.bg/en/post/100402627/gergiovden-greenery-lamb-and-merrymaking.

Bezovska, Albena and Petcova, Rossitsa (trans.). "Places of spiritual power in Bulgarian folk traditions." May 17, 2013. http://bnr.bg/en/post/100154045/places-of-spiritual-power-in-bulgarian-folk-traditions.

Boteva, Dilyana and Fol, Alexander (ed.). "The Heros of the Thracian Iconic Narrative: A Data Base Analysis" Sofia, pp. 817 – 821. Sofia: Institute of Thracology – Bulgarian Academy of Sciences, 2002. http://www.academia.edu/1371003/The_Heros_of_the_Thracian_Iconic_Narrative_A_Data_Base_Analysis.

Dimitrova, Nora. "Inscriptions and Iconography in the Monuments of the Thracian Rider." Hesperia 71, pp. 209-229. American School of Classical Studies at Athens, 2002.

Ezlink. "Thracian Gods." http://www.eliznik.org.uk/Bulgaria/history/thracian-gods.htm.

HostingUK.com. "The Bulgarian Festival Calendar - Saint Dimitrius of Salonika." http://12121.hostinguk.com/dimitrius.htm.

Konstantinova, Daniela (trans.). "Dimitrovden (St. Demetrius Feast)." Oct. 24, 2013. http://bnr.bg/en/post/100218345/dimitrovden-st-demetrius-feast.

Konstantinova, Daniela (trans.). "On St. George's Day." May 4, 2012. http://bnr.bg/en/post/100152278/on-st-georges-day.

Krachunova, Mariyana. "Krali Marko-Bulgarian legend." March 22, 2009. http://twinblog.etwinning.net/8383/posts/?CSATCQAZBWAVBU.

Liapis, Vayos. "The Thracian Cult of Rhesus and the Heros Equitans." Kernos 24 (2011), pp. 95-104. http://www.academia.edu/1024089/The_Thracian_Cult_of_Rhesus_and_the_Heros_Equitans.

Markov, Alexander (trans.). "Dragons and Lamias in Bulgarian folklore." May 31, 2013. https://bnr.bg/en/post/100200249/dragons-and-lamias-in-bulgarian-folklore.

OMDA Ltd. "The Traditional Bulgarian Orthodox Marriage in the Past." http://www.omda.bg/public/engl/ethnography/svatba_engl.html.

Petcova, Rossitsa (trans.). "Cold winter and heavy snow in Bulgarian folklore." Feb. 22, 2013. http://bnr.bg/en/post/100187648/cold-winter-and-heavy-snow-in-bulgarian-folklore.

Petcova, Rossitsa (trans.). "Dimitrovden - the day of Saint Demetrius." Oct. 26, 2010. http://bnr.bg/en/post/100113316/dimitrovden---the-day-of-saint-demetrius.

Plovdiv Guide. Traditions & Name Days - Dimitrovden (St. Demetrius's Day) - October 26." http://www.plovdivguide.com/_m1703/Traditions-Namedays/DIMITROVDEN--St-Demetriuss-Day---October-26-580.

Sanctus Sabazios. "Thracian Sabazios: 'The Fire of Heaven.' " http://www.sabazius.com/thracian-sabazios.html.

**Arkhangelovden**

Baeva, Vihra and Daynova, Milena (trans.) "Legends of Archangel Michael and the army of angels." Nov. 8, 2014. http://bnr.bg/en/post/100481665/legends-of-archangel-michael-and-the-army-of-angels.

Bezovska, Albena and Atanasov, Kostadin (trans.). "Details and facts about Bulgarian family services and religious sacrifice." Aug. 31, 2014. http://bnr.bg/en/post/print/100453885/details-and-facts-about-bulgarian-family-services-and-religious-sacrifice.

Bezovska, Albena and Markov, Alexander (trans.). "Day of Saint Michael the Archangel – commemoration of the departed." Nov. 14, 2011. http://bnr.bg/en/post/100129671/day-of-saint-michael-the-archangel-commemoration-of-the-departed.

Bezovska, Albena and Petcova, Rossitsa (trans.). "The windmill: legends, beliefs and folk songs." Jan. 27, 2012. http://bnr.bg/en/post/100138440/the-windmill-legends-beliefs-and-folk-songs.

HostingUK.com. "The Bulgarian Festival Calendar - Michaelmas - Saint Rangel Day." http://12121.hostinguk.com/michaelmas.htm.

Konstantinova, Daniela (trans.). "Bread kneading, a Bulgarian tradition renewed." April 22, 2013. https://bnr.bg/en/post/100195314/bread-kneading-a-bulgarian-tradition-renewed.

Konstantinova, Daniela (trans.). "In the afterworld: folklore notions about afterlife." Nov. 7, 2013. http://bnr.bg/en/post/100220328/in-the-afterworld-folklore-notions-about-afterlife.

Milkova, Stiliana. "Walled-in Wives, Dragon's Brides, and Wild Fairies: Women in the Bulgarian Folk Tradition." In Forum Folkloristika, Eastern European Folklife Center. Inaugural Edition. Issue 1, Spring 2012. https://www.eefc.org/folkloristika_1-1.shtml.

Nikov, Nikola. "Holidays of the Bulgarians in Myths and Legends." http://www.promacedonia.org/bg_folklore/en/index.htm

Petcova, Rossitsa (trans.). "Legends and stories about famous Bulgarian master builders." Sept. 29, 2011. http://bnr.bg/en/post/100127631/legends-and-stories-about-famous-bulgarian-master-builders.

Petcova, Rossitsa (trans.). "Saint Archangel Michael." Nov. 5, 2010. http://bnr.bg/en/post/100113806/saint-archangel-michael.

Rossier, Darina. "Bulgarian Folklore: Talasuhm." http://www.learn-bulgarian.net/blog/bulgarian-folklore-talasuhm/.

Vuchkov. "Background to Bulgarian Myth and Folklore - The Thracians." May 31, 2005. http://www.network54.com/Forum/414186/thread/1117606591/last-1117606591/Background+to+ Bulgarian+Myth+and+ Folklore.

**Nikulden**
Baeva, Vihra and Daynova, Milena (trans.). "Like a fish in deep water – symbolism connected with fish in Bulgarian folklore and tradition." Dec. 6, 2014. http://bnr.bg/en/post/100491469/like-a-fish-in-deep-water-symbolism-connected-with-fish-in-bulgarian-folklore-and-tradition.

Bezovska, Albena and Konstantinova, Daniela (trans.). "St. Nicolas, Santa and the Bulgarian Nikulden." Dec. 6, 2013. https://bnr.bg/en/post/100178659/st-nicolas-santa-and-the-bulgarian-nikulden.

Find Bulgarian Food. "Bulgarian Namedays." http://www.findbgfood.com/namedays.htm.

OMDA: Wonderland Bulgaria. "Traditional and Modern Names Among the Bulgarian Christian Population." http://www.omda.bg/public/engl/narod/BULG_IME_en.htm.

Only in Bulgaria. "Bulgarian Name Days." http://www.onlyinbulgaria.com/bulgarian-name-days.htm.

Orgsites.com. "Bulgarian Holidays, Name Days, Orthodox Church Days, and Traditional Celebrations." http://www.orgsites.com/wa/facab/_pgg7.php3.

Plodiv Guide. "Traditions and NameDays." http://www.plovdivguide.com/_m1703/Traditions-Namedays/.

Rossier, Darina. "Bulgarian Holidays: Name Days." http://www.learn-bulgarian.net/blog/bulgarian-holidays-name-days/.

Wikipedia. "Saint Nicholas. http://en.wikipedia.org/wiki/Saint_Nicholas.

# About the Author

Ronesa Aveela is a freelance artist and writer who lives near Boston, MA. She likes writing mystery romance inspired by legends and tales. In her free time she paints. Her artistic interests include the female figure, Greek and Thracian mythology, folklore tales, and the natural world interpreted through her eyes. Ronesa visited Emona and the Black Sea in 1998. She was inspired to use her brushes and pen to depict not only Emona's beauty, but also the characters in the book—both born from the experience she had in this mystical place. Ronesa is married and has two children, a dog, and a cat.

# Ronesa's Books

*Mystical Emona: Soul's Journey*
*Light Love Rituals: Bulgarian Myths, Legends, and Folklore*

**Baba Treasure Chest series**
*The Christmas Thief*
*The Miracle Stork*
*Born From the Ashes*
*Mermaid's Gift*

**Adult Coloring Books**
*Mermaids Around the World*
*More Mermaids Around the World*

**Cookbook**
*Mediterranean & Bulgarian Cuisine: 12 Easy Traditional Favorites*

**Coming soon**
*The Unborn Hero of Dragon Village*

# Reviews

Please consider leaving a review to help indie authors. Thank you.

www.ingramcontent.com/pod-product-compliance
Lightning Source LLC
Chambersburg PA
CBHW042349030426
42336CB00025B/3428